From the Desk of a Dog Diva

By Tracie Laliberte

For my parents Paul and Thelma who have always understood the obsession

FROM THE DESK OF A DOG DIVA

ISBN 978-1530862481

Cataloging in Publication Data

Laliberte,Tracie.

·From the desk of a dog diva / Tracie Laliberte.

1 2 3 4 5 6 7 8 9 0
Printed in the United States of America

Contents

Introduction

"My name is Tracie Laliberte and I'm a dog addict. It has been less than 5 seconds since I have thought about dogs or picked dog hair off my clothes."
–Tracie Laliberte

Do you consider yourself to be more of a dog person or a cat person? Like many people, I have always believed that there is a huge difference between the two. I explain it as a sort of men are from Mars, women are from Venus comparison. Dogs are humankind's best friend, and cats, errr, well; they are aloof. As for me, I consider myself to be a devout dog person. Do not get me wrong, it is not that I don't have love for all of nature's creatures, it is just that if I was to be stranded on a desert island and forced to choose, I would definitely prefer to be in the company of dogs. In fact, if dogs weren't regarded as such a humble creature to humanity, I'd boldly proclaim myself to be a doggy elitist.

My name is Tracie, and simply put: I love dogs. I've had dogs my whole life. I bred and raised show dogs for the better part of my youth, and have worked in the dog profession for my entire adult life. I honestly cannot say that I remember a time in the past forty-something years when the first thing I did in the morning was not tend to the dogs. Most days, I take care of walking and feeding the pooches even before having my morning coffee.

As it is the case with many people, my doing ANYTHING before morning coffee means that it is some serious stuff. My life with dogs IS this kind of serious, perhaps even more serious than a Scooby Snack is to a Labrador Retriever. I work with dogs mostly all day, every day. Many evenings, I can be found either instructing dog training classes or giving lectures on the topic of dogs to various dog enthusiast groups. Although I once kept as many as thirty-five dogs, at the present moment I only have three travel-sized Cavalier King Charles Spaniels of my own. At least one of them accompanies me nearly everywhere I go on a daily basis: on errands, to work, and even to college where I'm working on a Doctorate of Philosophy as dog-lover turned serious academician. In the classroom, when I'm not smuggling one of them under the desk in a discrete doggy purse, the presence of dogs sometimes takes the form of tufts of dog hair that waft out from in-between the pages of my very serious textbooks. Guess what my dissertation topic is? Yes, that's right. Dogs. You could say that I give the expression "gone to the dogs" a whole new meaning.

In fact, my college peers were the ones who first began half-jokingly calling me a "dog diva" because in addition to having an abnormal love for dogs, I also have an affinity for wobbling across campus in insanely high heels. Early in my coursework, classmates learned that they could always count on me to somehow connect dogs to whatever particular subject we happened to be exploring at that moment. As a joke one time, they challenged me to make a connection between dogs and soup. I don't think that they were all that surprised when I recalled the story of how I used to train show dogs to hold their show poses by positioning their feet on the tops of soup cans. My peers also grew to understand that they could come to me for all sorts of advice and suggestions about those everyday problems they might be experiencing with their beloved family dogs as well.

Nevertheless, my academic life has inspired me to become a prolific writer on the subject of dogs, and my published work spans from formal scholarly journal articles and professional publications to mainstream newspaper columns and Internet blogs. My writing earned an Arthur award from the Alliance of Purebred Dog Writers in 2007 and several pieces have been nominated for the Dog Writers Association of America's Maxwell award in recent years. In 2010, I barked out loud when I learned that my work had been nominated for the AKC Responsible Dog Ownership Public Service Award.

The pages within contain short column articles on a spectrum of doggie subjects. These column articles were written twice monthly over a period of 4 years beginning in 2006. You will notice that the subject matter often coincides with a celebration or a current event. You will also see that there are many, many articles that were inspired by my own life circumstances or important personal concerns. Essentially, although my work is clearly devoted to humankind's best friend, this collection extends beyond being simply writings on the subject of dogs. If you read closely, you will find that woven into these pages is a four-year personal journey from the other end of the leash of my life with my canine companions.

When I began this particular writing journey, I was a bride of less than one year in 2006. Within a four-year span, I experienced some significant life events: My husband deployed to Iraq and returned, my dog died, I acquired a new dog and eventually two more, one of my parents became ill and I divorced by the end of 2010. By reading, you can see that throughout this relatively brief amount of time, humankind's best friends not only remained faithfully at the side of this dedicated dog diva, but they also served as my models, inspiration and conduits for storytelling. Each article is a kibble in the bag of my life; this is a life that is made whole by dogs.

Wags,

Tracie

Chapter 1: Dog Care

"Dogs have given us their absolute all. We are the center of their universe. We are the focus of their love and faith and trust. They serve us in return for scraps. It is without a doubt the best deal man has ever made." -Roger Caras

Photo by Tracie Laliberte

Nurturing from nose to tail

Dental Care

Years ago, I had a dog that smiled. My lovable "Whitney" was so happy that she walked around grinning at every person she met. In her younger years, she had a beautiful grille of pearly whites that won her many admirers. Unfortunately for Whitney, in those days we dog lovers didn't understand the importance of taking care of our dog's teeth. By the time Whitney was 10 years old, her supermodel smirk had sadly deteriorated into a goofy showing of gums.

Fortunately, in recent years the pet industry has responded to the various health needs that are associated with the modern lifestyle and increased life expectancy of our furry family members. Many of the serious dental problems once associated with diet and the accumulation of dog years can now be minimized with preventative measures started earlier in the dog's life.

The pet food industry has declared February National Pet Dental Health Month because industry professionals understand that healthy teeth and gums are just as important to dogs as they are for humans. Dogs not only need their teeth to eat, but they are also vital in the dog's ability to protect itself from harm.

Maintaining strong, clean teeth significantly lowers your dog's chances of developing painful gum infections that lead to tooth loss and cause other serious health conditions. Without regular cleaning, Fido's choppers accumulate tartar that causes bad breath and gingivitis. Ask your dog to open up and say "ahhh" while you play dental hygienist. If you see pasty yellow gunk on the teeth near the gum line, your dog has plaque and may need to visit the vet for an evaluation or to perhaps undergo a professional cleaning.

Once your dog's teeth are clean, it is easy to maintain a healthy bite. Routine brushing with fingertip toothbrushes and toothpaste that is specifically designed for dogs is one simple option. Remember, if you decide to go the toothbrush route, be sure to use doggy toothpaste. Human toothpaste is not meant to be swallowed, and teaching your dog to swish, gargle and spit seems pawsitively crazy.

Depending on your dog's chewing habits and jaw shape, there are a number of specially shaped knobby-covered chew devices available that help to stimulate the gums and floss away food particles. Crunchy dental treats are still another option.

Even more impressive are the next generation of animal oral care rinses. There are liquids that have been formulated to do an excellent job of loosening plaque and freshening breath. These enzyme rich products can be found in the form of daily drops that you add to your dog's drinking water, or you can find rinsing sprays that are applied directly to the teeth.

I'm more than happy to do whatever it takes to help my dog live a healthier life. And just for fun, I have placed his liver flavored toothpaste in the medicine cabinet. Can you imagine the expression on the face of my next bathroom snooping visitor? *–January 2007.*

Eye Staining

Anyone who owns a light colored dog knows how frustrating it can be to keep the hair around the eyes and mouth free from unsightly staining. White-coated breeds are especially prone, but any color dog may develop rust-colored channels on the inside corners of the eyes along the muzzle. A dog with fur staining may also have unsightly coppery discolorations around the mouth. Pooches that lick their feet might appear to be wearing brown socks.

People often make the mistake of thinking that their stained dog merely has a dirty face or paws and then become quite perplexed when they are unable to get Fido to look clean by simple shampooing. The fact is that no amount of scrubbing in the dog spaw will return stubbornly stained fur back to the original color. When left untreated, the discoloration generally deepens over time.

Eye staining has a number of underlying causes. Teething puppies or dogs with blocked tear ducts will often overproduce tears that moisten the hair at the corners of the eyes. Bacteria and yeast breed in these wet corners and their microbial waste products tinge the hair orange. Similarly, dogs with ear infections or those with allergies also experience excessive tearing that causes stains.

Eliminating discoloration that results from allergies or infections is a matter of treating the underlying condition and keeping the corners of the eyes as clean and as dry as possible. Frequent face washing with a warm moist cloth followed by thorough drying helps to minimize staining while the underlying condition is being treated medically.

Nevertheless, even dogs in perfect physical condition can exhibit severe staining. If you notice that your healthy dog has tangerine tinted streaks at the corners of the eyes, mouth or on the feet, there is a very good chance that he or she is drinking over-mineralized water or consuming a dog food that contains beet pulp. In these cases, the stain is being transmitted through the dog's body fluids. Drooling causes stains on facial hair and licking the paws or performing personal hygiene causes saliva to discolor the fur on other parts of the body.

You can eliminate the sources of these stains by making sure that you are providing a beet pulp free diet and by topping off the water bowl with distilled water. Please note that bottled or filtered water and distilled water are not the same. You must use distilled water to stop the stain. This type of water is available at most grocery stores.

Bear in mind that once you begin treating stained coat, the fur will not magically turn back to its original light hue overnight. Stained hair must grow out and eventually be replaced by the dog's naturally colored coat. –*January 2010*

Skin Allergies

You hear it as staccato background noise during dinner: Thump-thump-thump-thump. It is not the boom of rap music. It is the beat of your dog's leg knocking on the floor as she scratches behind her ear. It's there again in the dead of night disturbing you from a gentle dream: swish-swish-swish-swish. It's not some reggae whisk. This time she's lapping at her feet. These are the annoying sounds of allergies.

Most veterinarians agree that allergies are the most common condition that affects dogs. Excessive scratching, runny eyes, inflamed ears, sneezing and even digestive disorders may be signs that your dog is suffering from allergies.

Explaining that your dog has allergies is another way of saying that your pet's immune system has kicked into overdrive to rid the body of something that it doesn't like. These undesirable substances, called allergens, can be found in the outside environment or can occur within the body. Sometimes allergens are inhaled like pollen or ingested in the form of foods. Bacteria, parasites or other substances that come into contact with the skin can also cause allergic reactions.

Like we humans, some dogs suffer from seasonal allergies. Spring and fall can be particularly bothersome to animals that are sensitive to molds, mildew, pollen, trees or leaves. If you notice that your dog itches or bites at her skin more during certain times of the year, chances are good that she has environmental allergies. Of course, your dog may be allergic to fleabites, so be sure to consider this possibility when screening for potential allergens.

If your dog habitually licks and chews at reddened paws, or has inflamed ears that may or may not be infected, she might be suffering from diet-related allergies. Many dogs are allergic to wheat gluten and some types of preservatives or artificial ingredients that are commonly added to commercial dog food. In most cases, switching to a higher grade feed, adding vitamin supplements or opting to go with a raw diet will eliminate dietary allergies altogether.

A veterinary visit is useful to diagnose all types of allergies. Treatment for reactions to contact or inhaled allergens from the environment may involve therapeutic baths, antihistamines or antibiotics. The first step in treating dietary allergies is to conduct at-home food ingredient testing.

Unfortunately, a dog can develop allergies at any time during her life. Signs such as licking and scratching should not be ignored because they are often the first signals of underlying issues. Untreated or ignored symptoms can quickly become greater problems such as severe skin infections. And, allergies can worsen with age. *–October 2008*

Anal Glands

People know that I am always willing to talk openly about a doggie's dirty little secrets. A friend of mine has a pooch named "Emmy Lou Harris" who was experiencing some tushie trouble. Emmy Lou was dragging her nether regions on the floor so often that visits to the vet for temporary relief from her condition practically became part of her weekly routine. When my friend asked me for advice about her dog's anal glands, she was barking up the right tree.

The phrase "anal glands" is surely something that raises human eyebrows and makes dogs tuck their tails and run. These glands are small internal sacs located at either side of the canine anus that serve a few important physiological purposes. First, these small balloon-like organs contain a highly concentrated brownish fluid that has a unique odor for every dog. This pungently scented liquid is your dog's nametag in the wild. The reason why dogs commonly greet one another by exchanging hind-end sniffs is to ascertain the identity of one another.

Additionally, the fluid within the anal sacs serves to give your dog's waste an extra spritz of canine "cologne" that enables them to boldly mark their territory when they eliminate solids. Members of the animal interested community also argue that an important and overlooked function of the anal sacs is to help to lubricate the stool as it passes out of the body.

Problems arise when the glands become over-filled or when they fail to function properly. Tushie-scooting on the floor, chewing at the tail region, or constant licking of the posterior are all signs of anal gland discomfort. A veterinarian can diagnose the condition and gently express the glands to provide immediate relief. However, holistic veterinarian Martin Goldstein explains that routinely emptying these sacs that are not designed to be empty "only increases the prospects of inflammation and impaction."

Emmy Lou was experiencing a chronic problem with over-filling, which is not uncommon in smaller breeds. My friend wanted to know if I knew of any natural alternatives to the constant manual expression of Emmy's glands. I told her that many professionals suggest increasing the amount of fiber in a dog's diet. This serves to bulk up the stool and puts added internal pressure on the sacs when the dog does its daily constitutional.

Following my advice, my friend started sprinkling whole grain breakfast cereal over Emmy Lou's breakfast and added snacks such as apples, green beans and carrots to her diet. Within a month, the results were noticeable. My friend told me that her princess ceased doing her embarrassing hind-end hustle across the floor, and she hasn't had to visit the vet for heiney-help since starting her high-fiber diet. Gives new meaning to the term ruffage, doesn't it? – *January 2008*

Stool Consumption

It's high time that someone barks the unbarkable about the secret lives of dogs. This skeleton in the closet is never the topic of conversation at cocktail parties. We don't even dare talk about this dirty habit even behind closed doors. As far as we humans are concerned, it is our doggie's deepest, darkest secret that is only ever delicately whimpered into the ears of sympathetic dog experts when they bring up the topic. I'm talking about the dog's habit of consuming its own stools. Yes, that's right. I'm referring to the dog that likes to "chew on its own poo."

This habit is more common than you might think. So much so that there's even a scientific name for the condition: it's called corprophagia. Its exact cause and cure continues to elude many dog experts. There are a few possible explanations for what initiates poochie poop scooping which, in turn, often causes it to become a bad habit.

Some authorities assert that certain dogs have a genetic predisposition to clean up after themselves. Others believe that the dog is simply trying to help humans keep the yard clean. We are to assume that if dogs had opposable thumbs they'd use the pooper scoop, but since they don't, they pick-up the only way they know how. My own theory is a bit different.

I have noticed an increase in this habit among dogs of all breeds in every size with the changes in dog food qualities and choices. The dog eats food based on the way that it smells rather than the way that it tastes; this is why it is so easy to poison a dog. Thus, I suspect that a combination of the individual dog's digestion and the particular diet that they consume causes them to eliminate droppings that may have what the dog considers to have a gourmet odor. To the dog, these goodies are worth a second look at the outdoor buffet.

If your dog does partake in this secret sin, no doubt you have tried a number of quick-fixes to make your dog understand that the doo-doo is a don't. You've probably tried sprinkling your dog's food with meat tenderizer, chlorophyll tablets or specially formulated powders only to find that in many cases these deterrents only work as long as you are using them. Some suggest following your dog around the yard and sprinkling a few drops of Tabasco sauce on fresh piles to try and deter the dog's sniff of interest.

My suggestion: sometimes a simple change in the choice brand of food you are feeding your dog is enough to eliminate stool scoffing. And, if you are going to be in the yard with Tabasco sauce anyway, why not simply remove and dispose of those piles before they become something of notice for your dog to devour? I always say that the best way to break the habit is to begin by removing the cause. Let's face it, I'm sure that dogs would agree that eating those frozen poopsicles that we have outside in this winter cold are more appropriately a warm weather treat anyway. –*February 2007*

Heartworm Prevention

When I was in the fifth grade, I won first place in the school science fair with my project on the life cycle of heartworm in dogs. Back in the mid 1970's, it was not uncommon for dogs to contract and die of heartworm disease. This was due to the fact that most dogs lived outside year-round with nothing but a hay-filled dog coop to escape the elements and routine veterinary care was practically unheard of. As I remember in our rural neighborhood, a dog would be considered lucky and quite privileged to get off its chain and go for a ride in the car just so the vet could jab it with a needle for a rabies vaccine.

Fortunately for our four-legged friends, the expectation for the quality and frequency of vet care is much different now. Routine care not only includes a yearly vaccination series, but diagnostic testing and preventative treatment as well. Incidentally, spring is usually the time of year when dogs are tested for heartworm disease.

Heartworm is a sickness that is spread when an infected mosquito bites a dog. The sting of the mosquito deposits microscopic larvae, or baby worms, in the dog's blood. Once they are within the bloodstream, the larvae begin to grow into bigger worms that settle into the animal's heart. It takes approximately six months for the microscopic larvae to reach the full-grown stage and adult worms can live for 7 years.

Over time as worms grow and the dog is exposed to the bites of other infected mosquitoes, the heart may become infested with worms. Adult worms in the heart of a dog interfere with blood flow more and more as they clog the heart's chambers and infiltrate the lungs. In severe cases, the dog may show signs of labored breathing and it may develop a mild or moderate cough. A dog with heartworm may also lose weight or be reluctant to exercise normally. Extreme infestations cause death.

The best treatment for the disease is prevention. A dog must first be tested to ensure that it is free from infection, and then it may take medication that disrupts the growth cycle of the worm. Preventative medication is available in daily or monthly tablets and chewable pills. An owner might also choose from monthly topical treatments that prevent infection by being absorbed through the skin.

Be sure to consult with your veterinarian if your dog is a Collie, Shetland Sheepdog, Australian Shepherd or Old English Sheepdog. These breeds of dogs sometimes have a gene defect that causes them to have a toxic reaction to the drug Ivermectin, a common preventative for heartworm. Any dog can be tested for sensitivity or you may decide to choose a different preventative medication to treat your pet.

Ears up dog lovers! Although it is less common, cats can contract heartworm disease too. Be sure to share this biscuit of information with the cat keepers in your life and be sure to have your pets tested this spring. *–April 2010*

Shedding

When I saw my diva with what I thought was a plush toy, but turned out to be a gigantic furball that had rolled out from under the sofa, I realized that spring is upon us. Unlike most people who anticipate Red Sox spring training or blooming daffodils, for me the arrival of spring means stocking up on Swiffer sweeper pads and buying lint rollers in bulk. Ask any dog owner and they will tell you that spring doesn't just mean the coming of nicer weather: it is a season that includes five weeks of excessive shedding and a renewed appreciation for beige clothing.

Dogs shed because their fur grows and falls out in a cycle that is triggered by ambient temperature and exposure to daylight. In the fall, the dog's hair will normally shed and then will grow in denser to insulate the dog during the cold winter months. In the spring, this abundant winter coat drops off and is replaced with a shorter and thinner coat that is more appropriate for warmer months. Granted, the domestic housedog is exposed to artificial light and a lifestyle that causes it to shed year-round, but even the best-kept house pet will still experience excessive spring seasonal shedding.

Luckily, modern science has come up with ways of managing the canine shedding cycle. There are tools, potions and other methods for keeping your house from looking like a yarn factory during spring shedding. Increasing your dog's fatty acid intake by providing daily nutritional supplements is a good place to start. I give my dogs a daily dose of salmon oil during spring months to support skin and coat health.

Regular brushing helps to remove excess fur, but it often isn't enough to free up that pesky undercoat which is mostly responsible for the springtime hair explosion. I recommend investing in a good quality shedding eliminator tool that is designed to remove the short invisible undercoat. A few hours of combing on a Saturday afternoon with one of these fine-toothed rake tools can really work miracles.

Specially formulated shed-stopping shampoos and conditioners can also help to loosen up hair that is about to shed while fortifying new hair growth. They smell delicious and are gentle on dog's skin. The trick is to be sure to brush your dog immediately following the bath to remove the loosened hair rather than letting it naturally collect on your favorite area rug.

One of my preferred methods for shed management is to place t-shirts on my dogs in-between brushings. I find this really helps to keep excess hair off of my furniture and clothing. Dressing my dogs in cute outfits also has corollary benefits. It not only decreases my lint-roller mania, but it also makes me think my dogs are so adorable that I simply don't care if I happen to find a stray hair stuck to my fork during dinner. –*April 2009*

Nail Grinders

Have you seen the latest in grooming gizmos? The newest fad in dog devices is this neat little tool that is designed to give the perfect poochie pawsicure. I saw an ad for one on a late-night television infomercial and was quite impressed with how simple nail trimming appeared to be in the commercial.

Basically, this gadget is a straight handle that is topped with a battery operated spinning wheel of sandpaper that is designed to smooth away the sharp edges of canine claws. It is the layperson's affordable version of the nail grinder that the professionals have been using for decades.

The commercial was very convincing and I'm sure a number of viewers reached for their credit cards with well-intentioned visions of filing away the ragged toenails of their feisty Fido. As I watched, I gave a giggle and remembered the woman with the "big black bag" who attended a recent presentation that I gave on the topic of at-home grooming.

Before my grooming presentation began, I noticed a woman enter the lecture hall carrying a rather large black handbag and I admired her style since big bags are the current fashion. After the program ended, I recognized this trendy woman by her purse as she approached me with a question. She wanted to know if I could comment on her grooming tools, and she began to heap the contents of the big black bag onto a table.

Her bag wasn't a handbag at all, but rather it was an oversized tote that she had stuffed with all the new-fangled grooming gizmos that she had been gathering for the past couple of years. As she held up tool after tool while insisting, "this doesn't work," I nodded in agreement and explained why each tool was flawed. We both ended up laughing at the thought of how much money she had invested in her bag of dog tricks that was really filled with empty promises of grooming miracles.

To be sure, nail grinders can be excellent tools for trimming and smoothing toenails. The fact remains, however, that the average pet owner experiences difficulty getting their beloved bow-wow to cooperate for a basic at-home nail trimming with conventional clippers. Now imagine asking these pooches to hold their paw steady while poking a single toenail through a pencil eraser sized safety opening as the nail trimmer makes a scary buzzing noise and creates a strange vibration on Fido's foot.

Perhaps you are thinking about purchasing a pet nail grinder for yourself or as a gift for your favorite dog-lover. Before spending your biscuits, remember that for this gadget to work as effectively as it does in the commercial, a dog should first be accustomed to having its nails trimmed at home. If the dog will not cooperate for a simple clipping, then chances are good that this trendy piece of technology will end up in the kitchen junk drawer.

Meanwhile, if you need a gift idea for someone whose canine companion does not comply with at home grooming, perhaps consider purchasing a stylish big black bag. These can be very useful for carrying dog treats. –*November 2008*

Ear Care

Listen up people! Today I'm going to sound off about your dog's ears. At a close second to the heart, the ears are my favorite part of the dog. Whether they are floppy, pointy, pendant, crooked, furry, or smooth; I love them all. And though many people may argue that the dog really listens with its heart, the fact is that the ears are a sophisticated canine apparatus designed to hear "I love you" back from their adoring two-legged fans.

According to a recent poll of veterinary clinics nation-wide, ear infections are the second leading cause of non-routine visits to the doctor. Infections of the ear can be extremely painful for your dog, and when left untreated they can lead to deafness. The wet weather of spring often contributes to a sharp rise in the incidence of ear afflictions, so hear this: you should make ear-checks a part of your daily doggy routine.

Ear infections can take the form of bacteria, fungus, mites or yeast. Discharge can range from yellow pus to chunky or grainy black debris, and early symptoms often take the form of head shaking or ear scratching. In more severe infections, even the most stoic dogs will cry when you touch their ears while petting their heads. Infected ears often have a horrible "stink" that is sometimes mislabeled as a dog's need for a bath.

Check your dog's ears daily by looking inside them. A healthy ear should be clean and the skin should look pink. Discharge or inflammation may be signs of trouble. You should clean your dog's ears weekly with white vinegar or specially formulated ear cleaners for dogs. Use soaked cotton swabs to clean only the parts of the ear that you can see. A normal healthy ear produces small amounts of wax that evaporate on a daily basis. Ideally, your dog should have minimal wax build up, if any at all. Wax over-production caused by food allergies or un-evaporated build-up can lead to infections. If your dog is maxi-waxy, clean regularly and try flapping your dog's ears open to allow the a-i-r to get into the e-a-r at daily intervals.

Damp ears can also create an optimal breeding ground for bacteria. As a rule, keep your dog's ears as dry as possible. Use a towel to wipe ears that have just come in from the rain, and use a hair dryer on medium to dry the inside ear-canal area after a bath. Remember that not all dogs are fond of air blowing in their ears, so this move is something that your dog has to be trained to cooperate with. My pooch sees the dryer and immediately rests his chin on the floor for some bonding with the blower.

If your dog does develop an infection, seek veterinary attention right away. The vet will examine the discharge and prescribe medication. To prevent a relapse, be sure to follow the instructions exactly. One more tip: If you do have to put drops in your dog's ears, make the experience more pleasant by warming the medication slightly. Do this by holding the bottle in the palm of your hand for 5-10 minutes. *–May 2007*

Forego Fireworks

When we heard the claps of thunder in the wee hours of the morning a few weeks ago, I began thinking about summer. The more the sky boomed the more I smiled, but the closer my dogs pressed against me. When I saw the youngest of my three King Charles Spaniels stick her head under the covers, I giggled. This reaction was certainly an improvement on last year's attempts to wrap herself around my neck like a scarf during storms. Still, it was clear that the loud noises were making a not so welcomed impression on my otherwise well-socialized doggy divas.

I was smiling because the thunderstorms made me think about all the dog-friendly fun stuff that comes with the warmer weather: daily walks, visits to the park, and endless fetch sessions in the back yard. The dogs, I'm sure, were reminded about those wretched city fireworks that I just supported by donating their monthly allowance of toy money. Talk about adding insult to injury.

Although we humans find them to be great fun, as far as most dogs are concerned there's probably nothing worse than being dragged to a fireworks display or city parade. Even the most well-socialized and emotionally stable dog is unlikely to get as excited about these summer celebrations as we humans do.

Think about it. Summer parades usually occur during the hottest time of the day with large groups of tightly packed, loud and rambunctious families. Dogs are expected to sit still on the hot concrete during commotion overload for hours. People step on their feet or tails and children scream in their ears. At the same time, the dog gets bumped and pushed by those around them. What's worse, the short leash they are on prevents them from doing what they really want, which is to make tracks for the air-conditioned comfort of the living-room sofa where they would prefer to bark at the parade through the front window.

Attending fireworks displays are ten times worse than parades for dogs. The noise from fireworks panics most dogs because they are extremely sensitive to sound. Only a few breeds of dogs were developed to ignore loud noises, such as hunting dogs. However, even when training a gun dog the hunter always exposes the dog to the sounds of firing guns gradually and with lots of control and positive reinforcement. In fact, every hunter begins training by first sitting with their prospective four-legged partner in the comfort and safety of the car with the windows rolled up during their initial exposure to the sounds of blasting gunfire. I would imagine that for a dog, a fireworks display feels much like sitting in the middle of a high-powered automatic weapon firing range.

Additionally, a bad experience with loud noises can create lasting negative associations that can lead to behavioral problems.

Friends of mine who live in a city that is well-known for its fireworks displays once told me how their dogs became terrified of thunder after being exposed to the close range sound of fireworks while sitting on the back deck. Dog professionals suggest that the best place for your dog to be during skyrockets in flight is safely inside the home. It helps to turn on the television or radio to drown out the booming and cracking noises outside.

To be sure, it is a rare dog that is able to sit calmly and ignore live fireworks exhibits. In spite of what you might think, the sidewalk parade is not the social event of the season in the dog's mind. In summer, be a kind and responsible dog owner by leaving your dog at home for these events. Celebrate by bringing them back a hot dog. *–May 2010*

Eye Care

I always enjoy learning new things, and I can honestly say that even after 35 professional years with dogs, there isn't a day that goes by when I don't gain some new knowledge about my four-legged friends. While attending a recent lecture about managing dog eye injuries, I learned some new and interesting things about the dog's eye.

The eye of the dog is different from a human eye in a few ways. The first is that unlike humans, dogs don't have a shelf-like bone in the lower part of the eye socket to protect the eyeball. This means that sometimes when a dog chews on sticks or other sharp objects, there is a chance that a splinter could penetrate from the back of the mouth up into the space behind the eye. Foreign matter behind the eye can lead to an infection or inflammation that causes the eye to swell or protrude. This condition can be detected early by simply looking down at your dog's eyes from the top of the head and noticing any imbalance in the position of the eyes in relation to the skull.

Another way that the dog's eye differs from people is in the dog's ability to retract the eye into the orbit. When a dog squints, it is actually using an eyeball muscle that pulls they eye further into the head and out of harm's way. A sunken eye is normally an indication of pain. Dry eyes, scratches on the eye or having something in the eye can cause discomfort that leads to retraction. Any narrowing of the eye should be immediately addressed by visual examination and followed by a gentle flushing with human grade saline solution. If squinting persists, you should take your dog to see the vet within 24 hours for proper diagnosis and treatment that may ultimately save your dog's vision.

It is vitally important that owners make a casual examination of their dog's eyes daily to check for health. Healthy eyes should be clear, moist and bright. Dogs that squint, behave like they can't see or have one or more protruding eyes should make an immediate visit to the vet. Unfortunately, owners too often ignore symptoms of chronic eye conditions, thinking they are not serious because they don't look like an emergency. Nothing could be further from the truth, as untreated symptoms can easily become eyenormous problems that are painful to both the dog and the wallet.

Personally, I cannot help but look deeply into the eyes of my dogs daily. Aside from forever wondering what kind of intelligence lies behind those mysterious dark globes, I know how important healthy eyes are for a dog's overall well being. After all, whom else could I depend on to serve as my personal team of seeing-eye dogs if I were to lose a contact lens? *–October 2009*

Coat Brushing

While shopping at a local pet superstore this week, I overheard an owner pleading with the groomer not to shave her dog. "I want her to have a puppy cut," I heard the owner whine. Out of the corner of my eye, I glimpsed the woman clutching a matted pint sized pooch that looked like a bleached version of Bob Marley.

As she leaned over fingering at the dreadlocks, the groomer responded, "I'm sorry, but she's so matted that I really don't think that I'll have any choice but to clip her short." The owner barked, "You CAN'T shave her! The last time I had her groomed, last year, the groomer traumatized her by cutting her bald and she looked like a rat. I WANT her to have a puppy cut."

This scene made me wonder why dogs don't bite their owners for not taking better care of them. The fact is, no matter how much this woman wanted to accuse the last sympathetic groomer of traumatizing her dog; I'd be willing to bet that the owner herself was one-hundred percent at fault for not brushing her dog in-between groomings.

"You don't blame the vet when your dog has to have teeth pulled, do you?" I wanted to howl from across the aisle. Then why blame the groomer for shearing the pelt off of your dog? My own experience tells me that shaving a dog is much worse for the groomer in terms of being concerned for not cutting or burning the skin of a stressed-out animal who isn't groomed often enough to understand the importance of being still when someone is operating a razor near your face.

So what if your dog doesn't like to be brushed? You wouldn't either if every time someone came near you with a grooming tool in his or her hand it became a hair-pulling session of agony. The trick is to brush your dog often enough so that grooming becomes a pleasurable activity. Personally, I brush my furry companions twice weekly while watching my favorite TV sitcoms: one half hour per brushing per dog.

All you need is a good soft-bristled slicker brush, a comb and an old towel to get started. Have your dog lie down on the towel, and begin to brush gently in layers starting at the skin and moving outwardly toward the ends of the hair. Be sure to spend a few extra moments behind the ears, under the elbows and at the hindquarters. Follow the brushing with a quick comb-through to be sure that you haven't missed any hidden knotting or retained hair that has been shed.

You may have to start off slowly and praise lavishly at first until your dog learns that a healthy brushing session feels like a massage. At my house, my two coifed canines jockey for position whenever they see the tools on the coffee table.

As for the woman in the superstore, I overheard the groomer graciously suggest that she promptly either buy her dog a sweater, or buy herself a brush. *-November 2007*

Holiday Care

The sight of giant snow globes on front lawns and the clog of sale flyers in my mailbox are clear indicators that the holiday season is chasing me. I've got lists to make, goodies to bake, and gifts to buy. Then there's the tree, the decorations, the lights, and of course there's the all-important task of puppy proofing my Christmas.

My howlidays should be doubly fun this year because my little elf just turned eight months old, and she will be at the peak of her puppy obnoxiousness just about the time that Santa Paws is digging his way down my chimney. I'm already cringing at the not-so-sugar plum visions of her tearing the ornaments off the tree, drinking the water from the tree stand, and pee-peeing on the tree skirt. I know that this, and so much worse, is coming to town.

The holiday season is the most dangerous time of the year for dogs. I'm not talking about the kind of irreparable emotional harm that my puppy will insist has been imposed upon her by being safely abandoned at home while I am out battling tug-of-war for the last on-sale squeaky toy among the pit bulls of shoppers at the mall. I'm talking about the ho-ho horrors associated with the everyday celebrations that occur within our dog dens.

Mostly every dog owner is familiar with the toxic dangers associated with the consumption of chocolate by dogs. The darker the chocolate, the more dangerous it is. In fact, one square of baker's chocolate can kill a small dog. As a general rule, you should keep all chocolate away from any place where a dog might reach it. Use extra caution when receiving boxes or gifts that may contain chocolate. Don't put these gifts under the tree, and exercise caution by asking that all deliveries be secured safely away from pets.

Believe it or not, the sugar substitute Xylitol that is commonly found in many chewing gums and some flavors of Altoids (that make wonderful stocking stuffers!) is toxic to dogs. Just two squares of gum can cause a reaction in a 20 lb. dog, and higher doses can trigger seizures and liver failure. Similarly, raisins and grapes can cause kidney breakdown and macadamia nuts can cause dramatic muscle weakness. These are all treats that often adorn our holiday tables.

Mistletoe and Holly plants have toxic leaves and berries that can be extremely poisonous. I never send these plants to pet owners, and whenever I receive one, I play it safe by donating the plant to the local community center. Glass tree ornaments, angel hair, metal ornament hooks and tinsel can also severely damage and obstruct animal digestive systems. I don't use any of these, but if they are a must in your doghouse they should always be placed on high branches as far away from Fido's forepaws as possible.

My puppy puts everything in her mouth, and last week I caught her standing on the dining room table. Unfortunately, I missed the opportunity to make a correction because I was laughing too hard, so I'm sure she'll do it again. Aye Chihuahua, surviving the holidays will be a Griswold's adventure in my house this year. – *December 2007*

Kennel Cough

One of the most common questions that I am asked about dogs during the chilly winter months is whether or not our furry friends can catch colds and the flu from people. Although dogs and humans can pass a number of illnesses between one another, a phenomenon called zoonosis, the trading of colds and flu is not found on this list.

However, it is important to know that even though dogs cannot catch colds from people, they still can develop a canine version of the cold known as tracheobronchitis. We humans refer to this ailment as kennel cough, and sick dogs usually exhibit a dry, hacking cough that may or may not be accompanied by a runny nose and fever.

There are several different types of viruses and bacteria that either alone or in combination can cause kennel cough. This vast array of strains means that under the right conditions even the toughest dog may be at risk. Like the common cold in people, kennel cough is more prevalent in places where there is a bigger doggie public. Where people commonly catch colds at school, the doctor's office, or on a plane, dogs can be exposed to germs at training class, the vet's office, or even at the Bowser bed and breakfast. Hence, the name: kennel cough.

Simple exposure to the illness does not guarantee that a dog will get sick. Like the common cold in people, dogs that are stressed or have a weary immune system are more likely to become ill. Some types of kennel cough are not dangerous at all, and the annoying coughing might go away on its own without any antibiotics. Unfortunately, other strains are very powerful and can become deadly in a short period of time. Because of this, it is important to always have a coughing dog checked by a veterinarian.

The good news is that with the right treatment, an ailing dog is sure to make a full recovery in about a week. The bad news is that, although now immune and seeming perfectly healthy, this same dog can shed the virus for several months thereby exposing other healthy dogs to the illness. This is why the neighbor's dog that spends time at the dog park can spread the airborne disease to your dog that never leaves the yard. This is also why eliminating kennel cough is a tail-chasing endeavor for pet professionals.

Fortunately, vaccination can protect your dog against many strains of the canine cold. The first immunity is administered in the form of nose drops that can be given as early as two weeks of age without interfering with the natural resistance to other diseases that the mother provides. After the initial treatment, a dog can then receive regular booster shots to maintain immunity.

Prevention is the best protection, so be sure to ask your veterinarian about vaccinating your dog against kennel cough. – *February 2008*

Food Supplements

Several weeks ago, I engaged in a rather interesting debate with a fellow animal professional about feeding my dog.

While we were discussing my skinny dog with the poor appetite, he told me that it was my own fault. He vehemently argued that dogs that don't eat are little Fidostein monsters created by owner spoiling. To be sure, there are many brilliant dogs who have figured out that refusing a bowl of cardboard kibble will eventually get them some fresh roasted chicken breast. However, this is not always the case. Refusal to eat has many valid root causes that have nothing to do with spoiling.

After hearing his condescending laugh, I suggested to my peer that a dog that refuses to eat might be legitimately suffering from a nutritional deficiency that independently contributes to anorexic tendencies. Studies in dogs demonstrate the link between amino acids and appetite, proving that dogs will refuse food that lacks in nutritional value.

My experience with show dogs has also exposed me to the inside dish on breed-specific problems related to nutritional deficiencies. Some Great Danes, for example, have a genetic disorder that interferes with zinc absorption. Similarly, Nordic breeds such as Alaskan Malamutes and Siberian Huskies commonly develop zinc responsive dermatosis when they are stressed because they do not absorb zinc under intense conditions. Symptoms of this disorder include hair loss, skin flaking and thickening as well as lesions around the eyes, mouth or ears. The consumer is just beginning to learn about the value of vitamin supplements for their pets. In an article in *Veterinary Practice News*, veterinarian Tom Cameron describes the vital link between optimal cell function and optimum nutrient levels. Many illnesses, he claims, are linked to cell damage that occurs when cells are not operating at full capacity due to a lack of nutritional support. He suggests that all dogs require daily nutritional supplements regardless of the quality of their diets.

In the conversation with my fellow pet professional, I was flabbergasted when he reminded me that grocery store brands of dog food are considered just as nutritionally complete as higher end brands. He then suggested that I should fill the bowl and hold out for however long it takes until my skinny dog eats. Fortunately, I might be an honorary Italian. Though I am still working on finding the perfect diet and balance of supplements for my little orange pipe-cleaner of a dog, I continue to put down her meal and say "mangia!" with the anticipation that at some point she will clean her plate every time. –*February 2010*

Hot Weather Care

You always hear about the dangers of leaving your dog in the hot car during summer weather, but did you know that heat exhaustion from exercise in warm weather could be just as dangerous? I was reminded about the harm that can come from over-exertion in warm weather last week while throwing the tennis ball outside for my toy-crazy Cavaliers.

We go out for a romp around the big back yard every day that weather permits. My dogs know this, and I think they must set their little woofie wristwatches because they always start getting antsy right around late afternoon "run time." They whine and bounce around until they see me holding the tennis ball chucker that they got as a gift one Christmas. Once they see the chucker, my mild-mannered darlings become devil-dogs by screaming relentlessly and heaving themselves against the door that leads outside.

Once outside, my little dogs sound like buffalo stampeding the ground as they tear a few warm-up laps around the yard before the chuck fest begins. When they see me wind up and get ready to launch, they charge fast and hard in the direction that they think the ball will land. They are quite competitive, and while only one dog holds the ball for return, they all bolt back at full speed so they can be poised and ready for the next chuck.

I learned just how fun-obsessed my dogs were last week when they insisted I continue the game despite the heat. They over-exercised themselves, and surely would have been in danger of over-heating had I not intervened. Most people think that dogs have the good sense to stop strenuous activity when they get too hot, but this simply is not true. Many dogs that love to run or play will think nothing of endangering themselves in extreme heat -- just to do what they love.

To prevent activity-related heat exhaustion, you should keep a watchful eye on your active dog in warmer weather. Remember, instead of sweating, dogs pant when they are hot. When you see panting that begins to get rapid or labored, it is time to stop the activity. It helps to limit activity to shaded areas and make sure there is plenty of fresh water available for your dog to drink. It is also advisable keep a kiddie pool filled ankle-deep with cool water close by to help your dog beat the summer heat.

Hot pooches can get quick relief from strenuous activity by being wet down with cool water. You should start by drenching their feet and bellies and work up toward their backs. Many dog professionals also use cooling jackets for dogs that work outside in warmer temperatures. This summer gear is great for pet dogs as well. The jacket should be drenched in water and placed over the dog before, during and after activity. Saturated coats can be frozen before use on really hot days. Basically they work by lowering the dog's core temperature much like sweating does in people.

My play-obsessed dogs will be happy to know that instead of hiding the ball until fall, I've just ordered them each a cooling jacket in fashion pink with custom embroidery that says "fetch." *–June 2010*

Auto Restraints

Imagine this: It is a warm summer's night. You and your dog are out for a ride in the car. The windows are rolled down, and the fresh breeze blows your ears back while you howl to your favorite summer song playing on the radio. You both cruise along the roadway without a care in the world.

Suddenly, you are jolted by an unfamiliar whooshing sound coming from behind you. You turn to look and all you see is the tail end of your dog hurling out the window of your moving car. You see your dog smack on the roadway, but you force your eyes forward to steer the car as panic sets in. When you look back again, the dog is gone.

Unfortunately, this horror story is not one of fiction. It happened in a nearby town a few weeks ago, and seeing the frantic owner just moments after losing her dog got me to thinking about the concern for safety when carting around our precious pooches.

Leaving your dog unrestrained while driving can be more dangerous than you might think. Aside from the obvious harm that can come to dogs if they jump out an open window, there are other concerns for safety as well. Dogs that ride with their heads sticking out the window are at risk for eye injuries from flying debris or neck injuries that can occur if the car suddenly stops short. Pets not safely secured may also be severely hurt in the event of an accident.

A free-ranging Rover can be the cause of accidents as well. Dogs that go on sight-seeing tours from the front seat to back seat, lunge at passing cars, or insist on riding on the driver's lap are serious distractions for drivers. In fact, according to a recent AAA study, pets are third on the list of worst in-car distractions.

Fortunately, there are many types of restraining devices available to keep pets safe while in transit. Crates and barriers keep dogs contained while still allowing them some freedom of movement. Seatbelt harnesses and canine car seats keep pets comfortably confined to the seat. These open restraints allow continued access to your pet and integrate easily with the safety gear that comes standard in every automobile.

Personally, I have always restrained my dogs while riding. My copilot, when she is not commuting in her crate, wears her safety harness. My backseat driver flirts with passing cars from a stylish lookout seat. And, on those occasions when the car top is down, they both wear sunglasses to protect their eyes.

People probably see me driving around with my canine cargo and think that my collar must be on too tight. Really, I'm just an over-protective dog mother. *–August 2008*

Hot Spots

Raise your paw if you are familiar with the doggy hot spot. Sorry, I'm not referring to some new Bow Wow Bistro or Doggy Discotheque. I'm talking about those awful puss-y yellow, sticky, stinky sores that can plague even the most pampered pets in the summer season. If your paw is still raised, and your stomach is not churning, read on for the skinny about how to halt hot spots.

While the exact cause of the hot spot can be elusive, there are some basic concepts to consider. Like people, every dog has a variety of naturally occurring bacteria both on and in its body that are harmless. The hot spot occurs when bacteria colonize and multiply exponentially on a dog's skin under the right conditions, causing an infection. Some dogs seem to be more prone to getting hot spots than others, and an increased susceptibility can suddenly appear at any stage in your dog's life.

Sometimes hot spots appear after an insect such as a mosquito or an ant has bitten a dog. Heat rash, itchy ears, and allergies are other common sources. Scratching or chewing the irritation can damage the outermost protective layer of the dog's skin, creating what is known as a route of entry for bacteria such as staphylococcus to set up camp. Summertime heat and humidity add to the problem because they enable the bacteria to multiply rapidly, which is why a small hot spot can become quite large overnight.

You can significantly decrease your dog's chances of getting hot spots by keeping Fido clean, dry and cool. A regular bath washes away dirt, allergens and keeps the skin's natural bacterial levels in check. Regular brushing removes shed hair and matting, which allows the skin to breathe in summertime heat. Most importantly, I recommend checking your best friend over daily as the perfect way to identify potential trouble spots early.

If your dog does develop a hot spot, wash the area well with soap and water, then dry the area thoroughly and apply some antibacterial creme. It also helps to clip the hair away from the affected area. Severe hot spots require the added help of an oral antibiotic that must be prescribed by your veterinarian.

If left untreated, hot spots can become really un-cool. I've seen cases where flies have laid eggs and the larvae have hatched on the dog's sore. If this doesn't sound like hot spot H--E--double chew sticks, then I don't know what does. –*August 2006*

Flea Prevention

I can appreciate my dog's sense of humor. I'll giggle if he streams my last roll of toilet paper all over the house when I'm not home. I'll laugh if he steals my sandwich off the coffee table when I'm not looking. I'll even give a chuckle if he parades around the dining room with my bras in his mouth when company visits. There is only one place where I draw the line: don't bug me. I have one simple rule. Fleas are unwelcome guests in my doghouse; this is no laughing matter.

Uggh. Fleas. It's hard to imagine that something as small as one-eighth of an inch can create such a circus. Most people think that once summer is over, the risk of their dog getting fleas is gone, and they foolishly stop using preventatives. The simple fact is that the fun is just jumping off for fleas in the fall season. Until the ground is frozen, the flea sees your dog as a cruise ship complete with midnight buffet and activities deck that sets sail from the chilly outdoors into the heated human home resort and spa.

According to the FDA, there are over 200 varieties of fleas. Do you want to know the joke? It seems that cat fleas are the main problem for dogs. Not that we need yet another reason to turn our noses up at cats, but cat fleas can live on cats, dogs, rabbits and they enjoy biting humans. There are some other flea facts that might bug you. Fleas only spend one quarter of their life on a host, the rest of the time they are in the environment and this insect can jump up to 2 feet. The life cycle of a flea can last anywhere from 2 weeks to 8 months, depending on environmental conditions. Fleas live on the blood they get from biting your dog and lay their eggs in blood, which look like little pieces of dirt on your dog's skin. A female, the bigger of the two genders, lays 15-20 eggs per day, up to 600 in her lifetime. A flea can live anywhere from 2 months to 1 year without feeding. I get itchy just thinking about this.

My advice: you should continue to treat your dog against fleas until the ground is frozen. Next generation topical treatments are the professional's first choices for combating fleas, but you can also use flea collars or pills that you can get from your veterinarian.

If you prefer, you may also go green by applying repellants such as a drop of lemon, rosemary, or lavender essential oil on your dogs collar.

My dog and I have an understanding. He tolerates that sticky stuff between his shoulder blades until my backyard is like the frozen tundra, and I laugh at his stupid jokes like forgetting the difference between sit and down whenever I attempt to demonstrate my skill as a trainer in public. –*September 2006*

Water

With so much focus on the important relationship between diet and a dog's health these days, the significance of water in canine well-being is sadly over-looked. Sure, the adage "you are what you eat" applies equally to dogs, but the fact that two-thirds of our dogs' bodies are composed of water should make us carefully consider how we hydrate our best friends.

Thankfully, the old habit of simply turning on the kitchen faucet and filling up the bowl is coming to an end. In fact, most concerned dog owners are choosing to dish out bottled spring or distilled water to all of their beloved pets. To be sure, purified water is a far better choice than stagnant tap water that tends to absorb the build-up of toxic components as it passes through old plumbing systems.

Yet, the problem still remains that commercial water is packaged in plastic bottles. Holistic health writer Juliette de Bairacli Levy explains, "Water sealed in bottles – plastic containers are especially bad – soon becomes lifeless and loses much of its health properties." She explains that water needs air in order to provide maximum health benefits.

The best water for the maintenance of whole health is free-running water that is protected from constant exposure to direct sunlight. But since very few of us have clear bubbling brooks in our back yards, small indoor water fountains provide an excellent healthful alternative. Fountains circulating with purified water are the chic city canine's dream. The trick is to be sure that the water bowl itself is stainless steel, glass or ceramic. Stone bowls are even better, and plastic or aluminum water dishes should be avoided altogether.

The vitality of the flowing fountain water can be further enhanced by placing a clean, smooth rock in the center of the drinking basin. The stone should be small, yet large enough so that a dog cannot pick it up or swallow it. This helps to supply water-soluble minerals and to keep the water cool.

You can further freshen the water by placing a small sprig of fresh rosemary beneath the rock. This herb is a way to naturally minimize impurities that get absorbed into the water from the surrounding environment.

If you decide to upgrade your dog's water supply, remember that you may have to teach Fido to drink from the fountain.

Thereafter, don't be surprised to find your darling spending most of its time hanging out at his or her new favorite watering hole. *–July 2008*

Toenails

Let's talk toenails. Although you might think otherwise, dog toenails are for more than just fluffing up the comforter before lying down. Toenails are an important part of mobility and propulsion; that is, moving from one place to the next and doing it quickly. They also enable the dog to hold its ground.

Like your own nails, your dog's toenails speak volumes about your pet. A dog with shorter nails on the front paws than on the rear paws most likely spends a fair share of time digging in the yard. Shorter rear nails means the dog is a chaser. Same length on all fours is the sure sign of canine royalty; these are the types of dogs that spend their days lounging on the sofa.

To be sure, one of my most favorite sounds is the delicate clicking of toenails across the kitchen linoleum. It brings life to my household. Sadly, it also means that my little prince needs a pawsicure. Like when administering heartworm prevention or applying flea and tick control, the general rule is that dog toenails should be trimmed back monthly.

For lack of a better metaphor, I liken the doggy toenail to a day-old jelly stick donut. The nail itself is the crunchy outside part, and the jelly represents what is known as the quick. The quick is composed of the nail's blood supply and nerve endings, which is why clipping a dog's nail too short makes a painful and bloody mess.

Using the jelly stick donut metaphor, you want to trim the crunchy donut part of a dog's nail just short of the jelly. Be sure to use a good quality nail clipper, and have someone help you if you and your dog are amateurs. Some dogs are foot sensitive and will not be too pleased as you play mad scientist while messing with their toes.

Try to have your dog lay on its back in a submissive position with your helper holding the dog's head and rubbing Bowser's belly. Trim a little at a time, one paw a day if necessary until you get the hang of it and have established a level of trust with your dog. Remember to praise your dog lavishly for every successful clip.

Your dog's toenails also speak volumes about you. Crow's feet toenails mean bad owner. Athletic length nails, or those which hover just a few centimeters above the floor when the dog is standing still, are a sign of love. –*June 2006*

Smoke-free Dogs

When I saw the truck pull up, I thought for a moment that my contact lenses had gone blurry because I could barely make out the outline of the driver in the smoke-filled passenger compartment of the vehicle. After he finished his cigarette, I watched the driver lead his dog out of the truck and at once the man and his dog both began coughing. When the man stopped hacking, he looked in my direction and started growling about his dog's allergies and snarling about all the money that he had wasted in vet bills for the dog's unresolved skin issues.

Because he did not ask for it, I forced myself to withhold my opinion in a controlled down stay. As he walked away with his still choking dog, I just shook my head and uttered under my breath: "talk about overlooking the obvious."

The surgeon general has determined that smoking and exposure to second-hand smoke is harmful to human health. It is so dangerous, in fact, that laws have been enacted to protect innocent people from exposure to this deadly substance. Most smokers understand the risks that cigarettes pose to themselves and to other people, however many smokers fail to recognize that second-hand smoke can be quite harmful to pets, too.

Studies have shown that dogs that live with smokers are more likely to develop cancer of the nose, sinuses and lungs than those dogs that live with non-smokers. Medium and long-nosed breeds are highly prone to cancer of the nose and sinuses because the toxins in tobacco smoke get trapped in the mucous membranes of nasal passages. Short-nosed breeds commonly develop lung cancer because more of the harmful chemicals present in smoke are breathed directly into the lungs. Inhalation of the 4,000 chemicals present in cigarette smoke is also linked with health issues of the eyes, skin, heart and reproductive system.

Similar to people, dogs can also experience allergic reactions by coming into contact with second-hand smoke. Smoke in the air gets trapped in animal fur and may be absorbed by the skin. Smoke-clogged hair and skin can cause a dog to scratch, bite and chew at its body. These reactions are commonly confused with allergies to food or environmental factors such as fleas. What's more, toxins can also be ingested when dogs lick at their coats or paws after walking or sleeping on smoke infused surfaces.

The good news is that the rising awareness of the negative impact of cigarette smoking on companion animals may provide incentive for smokers to quit. A recent survey by USA Today of over 3,000 pet owners revealed that smokers among the group would quit if there was strong and clear evidence that smoking might harm their pets.

If you smoke, please consider quitting for the love of your dog. – *August 2010*

Dangerous Chewing

As a youngster growing up with dogs, I learned to keep my favorite things out of the reach of chewing canine teeth at a very early age. As a teenager, this was kind of a cool thing for my mom; it meant that my room was always picked up and my clothes were always put away.

There are certain breeds of dogs such as Dobermans, Labradors and King Charles Spaniels that are known among dog professionals to be in touch with their inner goat. These dogs chew and ingest all sorts of items that should not be swallowed. As the owner of a breed of chew-obsessed pooches, I take extra precautions by always providing plenty of safe chew items and by keeping a constant watchful eye on my own little destructo pups.

My cautious concern came in handy earlier this summer while a friend's show dog was visiting me. One night, I was watching television in bed while surrounded by the dogs. One by one, they brought bones up on the bed and began chewing quietly when I realized that there was one more dog chewing than there were bones. Apparently my inventive chew diva had decided to improvise, and she was proudly gnawing on the television remote.

Believe it or not, every year the veterinary industry holds a contest to decide the winner among the x-rays of the most bizarre items that animals ingest. The majority of the contestants this year were Labs or Lab mixes that had swallowed a variety of items that included fishing hooks and telephone cords. This year's contest winner had swallowed 309 screws, nails and fence staples from a construction project.

No one can say for sure why it is that dogs eat things that they shouldn't. Sometimes it is because they are bored or anxious. Some believe that dogs eat personal items such as underwear, glasses, pens and remote controls because they smell like their favorite person. Others suggest that nutritional deficiencies cause dogs to eat stones and metal objects. No matter what the reason, eating foreign objects is dangerous and can be deadly.

Items that are not digestible can cause obstructions in the stomach and intestines. Even string and dental floss can wreak serious havoc by twisting around tissue in the intestines. Dogs that have blockages will often vomit, suddenly become anorexic and extremely lethargic or they may cough. These animals need immediate veterinary attention and often require emergency surgery.

I was really grateful to notice the television remote turned chew bone as soon as I did. I don't know what I would have done if Drew had swallowed it and the channel started to change every time she rolled on her stomach. –*September 2010*

Dangers of Tethering

My friends used to joke that I was some kind of human doggy homing device. They would swear that I could be standing in the middle of an empty field when out of nowhere a dog would suddenly walk up to me. Because I'm a magnet for dogs, I can't say that I was surprised when a loose dog found me in the neighborhood where my parents live a few weeks back. The worrisome part about this stray, however, was the fact that the wanderer was a Pit Bull who was not wearing a collar.

Before calling animal control, I decided to try and find out who owned the dog so that I could introduce myself and explain why it is generally a bad thing to allow one's Pit Bull Terrier - no matter how friendly - to roam residential neighborhoods. When I found the distressed owner, he explained that he had just recently adopted the dog. He also told me that earlier that day, his new four-legged family member had slipped out of the collar that was attached to a heavy-duty tie-out chain in the back yard.

When I saw how relieved this concerned owner was to have his dog back, I knew I'd have a good opportunity to explain why he shouldn't tie-up his new friend. Aside from the obvious dangers of having your dog returned to you by a nutty dog woman, escaped dogs can risk getting hit by cars and loose dogs cause mayhem that threatens people as well as other pets within a neighborhood.

Tethering itself can be equally as dangerous even for those dogs that don't break free. Some dogs that are tied up cannot escape harsh weather elements such as sun, wind or rain. Chains and lines can become easily tangled around stationary objects or twist and kink around the dog's legs and body. The weight of the chain pulling on a dog's neck not only puts the animal at risk for injuries, but it is also known to cause behavioral problems. Another overlooked danger, according to animal control advocate Carol Tyler, is that other animals can easily attack a dog that is tied-up.

States have begun to recognize the problems of tethering dogs and six states, including nearby Connecticut, have responded by enacting laws that regulate an owner's responsibility when it comes to tying out their dogs. Regulatory factors include the construction, size, weight and location of the tether; as well as the availability of shelter and the health of the dog. All of the state regulations include limits on the length of time that a dog may be restrained. At the local level, a growing number of communities are instituting bans on chaining altogether.

By the time we finished talking, the Pit Bull's owner agreed with my suggestion to install a fence for safely securing his new friend. I tried to convince him to include a doggy play area, puppy pool and spa within his proposed fencing project, but I don't think he went for it. Maybe he was worried that I might ask for some free doggy visitor passes as a reward for returning the lost dog. – *November 2010*

The Water Workout

This exceptionally snowy weather has really created some challenges for dog owners. Snow filled backyards and covered sidewalks mean that many of our dogs are lacking in outdoor exercise time. When one of my own dogs dashed up a snow bank along the eight foot stockade fence in my own backyard and placed her paws on the top of the fence as if to say "I could go over this if I really want to," I knew it was time to get busy offering the dogs some extra time doing our favorite indoor activities.

Against my mother's good advice, I throw the tennis ball inside for games of fetch. I regularly play hide and seek games by encouraging the dogs to "find" treats that I have cleverly hidden all over the house. Sometimes we do staircase relays by going up and down the stairs for no particular reason. Of course, they eventually figure out what I'm doing and sit at the top of the stairs giving me dirty looks while I hop up and down at the bottom cheering "come on down!" like a fool.

My latest bright idea came to me while reading about the health benefits of hydrotherapy for dogs. Exercising in water is one of the newest crazes for dogs. Water treadmills and swimming, activities that were once used primarily for injury rehabilitation, are now being promoted for canine exercise and sports conditioning. Water exercise is a wonderful aerobic activity that burns calories without straining the joints. Additionally, the resistance from the water builds strength in the muscles while improving flexibility, performance and posture. The warm water environment also provides added therapeutic benefits by soothing muscles and stimulating blood flow.

I must have been suffering from post-shoveling brain freeze when the idea of turning my old-fashioned claw foot bathtub into a doggy swimming pool swept over me. I thought that if I filled the tub to the top and used the doggy life jacket, I could hold my dogs in place one at a time while they swam away all of their excess energy. I thought this was such a brilliant idea that I immediately began filling up the tub.

When they heard the water running, the dogs vanished. They must have thought it was bath day even though I was hunting them down with a bright yellow life jacket in my hand. I found my first candidate for swim intramurals hiding in the closet pretending to be a pair of orange fuzzy slippers. Within an instant, I clipped on the flotation device and I began to gently submerge my dog feet-first into the tub of warm water.

I guess I should have measured the dog against the depth of the tub before I tried turning my bathroom into a sports center. The tub wasn't quite deep enough and instead of swimming, my diva just stood there in her silly lifejacket looking up at me with sheer disgust. She knew what was coming next. I reached for the bottle of shampoo since she was already three-quarters wet anyway. *–February 2011*

Preventing Frostbite

Did you see that crazy woman walking her little orange dog through the city in the freezing cold last week? She was the one wearing the earmuffs, mittens and a scarf wrapped around her face so that all you could see was her nose sticking out. The woman was power walking while cheering on her couch potato Cavalier King Charles Spaniel, who was just about keeping up the pace.

If you saw that lunatic, you saw me in the process of getting my show dog in shape for ring competition in the upcoming year. For the next several weeks, I will be the coach for my canine athlete in training. She's got to lose a pound of flab and firm up her thighs before the start of the show season, which means walking every day. Naturally, as the temperature grows colder I will be taking extra precautions to protect her from the danger of frostbite that is associated with the wintertime workout.

Just because a dog wears a fur coat does not mean that it can't get frostbite. Short-haired breeds, small dogs, wet dogs, those who remain outside for prolonged periods of time and dogs with sensitivity to the cold are all potential candidates for the problem of cold exposure. When a dog is exposed to the cold, it conserves heat by reducing the flow of blood to the body's extremities. When the peripheral parts of the body aren't kept warm by blood flow, ice crystals may form in the tissue, causing it to die. Hence, very cold weather can cause tissue damage to the ear tips, paws and tail.

Frostbite can be difficult to detect on dogs because the body is covered with hair, but the first sign is very pale skin that is extremely cold to the touch. As the skin warms, it will become very red and painful to the dog. Within a few days of frostbite exposure, the skin will become dry and scaly. In severe cases, the dead flesh will turn black and begin to peel away as infection sets in.

Dogs with suspected areas of frostbite should be treated immediately by gently warming up the cold skin. This can be done by placing the dog in a warm room, by wrapping it in a blanket, or by positioning a hot water bottle on those affected areas. Avoid dipping the dog in hot water, as this can further damage the skin. Also resist your urge to rub or massage the area, as this releases toxins that will also cause more harm to the already damaged tissue.

You can prevent frostbite by limiting the amount of time your dog spends outside in the bitter cold or snow. You can also put a jacket on your dog to help to maintain its core temperature, which keeps the blood flowing to the outer limits of the body.

On those wintry days that lie ahead, my furry little prizefighter will be wearing her pink jogging suit when we workout on the city sidewalks. If you see us, be sure to shout "Yeo" using your best Rocky Balboa impersonation. *–December 2010*

Feeding The Raw Diet

I first began thinking about the food that I offered to my furry family after the dog food recall a few years ago. I had always confidently fed food from a bag, but when I started learning more about what's really in dog food and investigating the nutritional needs of dogs, I very quickly realized that some changes needed to be made with regard to what I plopped into the dog dish.

Every where I researched, I found that dog nutritional experts unanimously advocate feeding a raw diet, but I just wasn't ready get past my own feelings of "ewwwww" at that point in time. In a compromise, I began home cooking for my pets. This definitely offered a higher quality alternative to processed foods, but the simple fact was this heat-damaged fare still didn't fully address the real nutritional needs of my dogs.

You see, even though we think of the canine as a domesticated animal, the truth is that our four-legged companions are really socially skilled descendants of the meat-eating wolf. In fact, the dog should be properly recognized as an opportunistic scavenger carnivore whose physical anatomy is testament to this designation. The dog has a hinged jaw that is made to pulverize, and they have sharply pointed teeth that are designed for ripping and tearing. In contrast, the herbivorous cow has a jaw that slides from side to side and flat surfaced teeth that are made for grinding hay and corn.

The dog also has elevated levels of hydrochloric acid in the stomach; this is specifically used for killing any bacteria that may be present in the fresh meat as it is consumed. Additionally, dogs have a short, smooth intestine which functions to move food through the body while absorbing nutrients quickly. Unlike the long and winding intestine of the omnivorous human, the dog's digestive system isn't physically designed for the time intensive process that is necessary to adequately digest grains.

Experts in dog nutrition who advocate raw feeding correctly remind pet owners that diet is the cornerstone of health. They explain that diets high in grains and cereals burden the digestive system, which can create internal toxicity. Similarly, nutritionally deficient diets set the dog up to develop future health conditions.

After finishing a book called "Work Wonders" by veterinarian Tom Lonsdale, I was finally convinced to begin feeding my dogs a species appropriate raw diet and I am amazed by how quickly my dogs have shown a significant positive response to a diet that now optimally meets their nutritional needs.

Of course, when my new kitchen meat grinder arrived in the mail last week, my oldest gave me a worried look as if to say "Surely I couldn't have been THAT bad?" She gave a sigh of relief when she saw me grind a chicken leg into her dinner bowl. *–January 2011*

Chapter 2: Training

"Every dog should have a man of his own. There is nothing like a well-behaved person around the house to spread the dog's blanket for him, or bring him his supper when he comes home man-tired at night"   -Corey Ford

Photo by Tracie Laliberte

Sit! Stay! Fetch Your Toothbrush!

Clicker Training

People are fur-ever asking me if I think that their dog is too old to learn something new. The fact is, even though an older dog may not learn as fast as a younger one, with a little patience and consistency it is absolutely possible to teach a dog new tricks at virtually any age.

Most people have difficulty training their dog simple concepts because their training approach is not positive, clear and consistent. Confused dogs can quickly become demotivated, or worse: they learn the easiest trick, which is convincing their humans that they are dummies.

A great approach to teaching your dog new tricks is to use the clicker training method. Basically, the clicker is a very inexpensive hand-held toy like device that works by making a crisp, clear "click" sound when you press the lever. The click sound is better than a human voice because it is predictable and consistent. Unlike a person, the clicker makes the exact same sound regardless of how it is feeling. The click sound also provides a clearer and more immediate marker for a specific behavior.

You should begin clicker training by teaching the dog to associate the click sound with getting a treat. Like Pavlov's drooling dogs, each time the four-legged student hears the click; it should be immediately rewarded with a yummy treat that acts as positive reinforcement. Once your dog learns that clicks mean treats, you can begin to use it to incrementally mark behaviors that you desire while working with one behavior at a time.

Let me explain. Say you want to teach your dog to wag its tail on command. Wait until you see your dog wagging and then immediately click and treat. The click will act as a bridge between the behavior and the treat. After a few times of rewarding the wag, the dog will begin trying to figure out which behavior is eliciting treats. As the dog starts to figure out that it is the waving tail, you should then begin to attach a cue word such as "wag" to this behavior. You may then transition to signaling the behavior with the word "wag." At this final stage, you click and reward to reinforce the sequence only when the dog wags its tail immediately after hearing the cue word.

Once the dog reliably wags its tail upon being signaled in any environment, it has learned the behavior and the clicker may be eliminated or used for teaching a new word.
Interestingly, scientists in Germany have confirmed that a dog can learn upwards of two hundred words. This is approximately equivalent to the vocabulary of a three year-old child.

Clicker training can be great fun and you will be amazed by how quickly and efficiently even the oldest dog can learn new tricks. Now if trainers can just figure out a method for clicker training husbands. *–March 2009*

Walking On-Leash

One of my most favorite visions is that of a person and their dog bounding down a sidewalk together. I feel especially scratched behind the ears when the pair is moving along at a perfectly complementary pace, and the two are tethered together by a leash that hangs like cooked spaghetti. Unfortunately, this type of teamwork seems to be the exception rather than the rule. We've all seen it: the dog dragging a person with arm fully outstretched and feet pounding one after the other as if ready to take flight like a human kite. Most on-lookers laugh and wonder just who is walking whom?

I can relate to this disruptive scene because I've had my share of clashes with unruly canines over the years. In these most recent five years, for example, I've broken both ankles on separate occasions, been bitten through the hand, and I have been knocked out - all while interacting with other people's rowdy dogs. Is there any wonder as to why humankind's best friend is allowed in so few public places in this country?

I believe these out-of-control canines are yet another symptom of our culture in chaos. American society is running amok with the pandemonium of personal conflict, mad material consumption, and outrageous acts of violence. And in coping with our renegade dogs, like with everything from the environmental crisis to gang-related mayhem, we struggle to "fix" the mess only when the problem becomes an emergency.

66

Many owners mistakenly try to meet their dog's simple challenge of walking politely on a leash by using quick-fix contraptions such as pinch collars, electronic shock collars or choker collars only to discover that they are no substitute for basic and consistent training. My advice: If you want your dog to walk courteously on a leash, you must first discipline yourself.

Walk your dog on a leash daily, even if it is just for a short trip to the mailbox. Begin your walk by commanding your dog to "sit" and then "heel" as you take one small puppy step forward. If your dog pulls, immediately freeze in your tracks and refuse to move again until the dog has stopped pulling. Once the dog eases up, show your approval and then begin the whole process again. This approach gives your pet the message that if he/she wants to proceed, it must be done with gentle restraint. When your four-legged friend does have a moment of civilized striding be sure to praise lavishly.

Be warned, your first field trip to the mailbox may take some time, so be certain to bundle up during this chilly time of the year. And don't give up! Before you know it, you'll be strutting gracefully with your doggy debutante around the block in an effort to walk off those extra pounds you've both gained from overindulging in cookies around the chaotic holidays. *–November 2006*

Coming When Called

The other day, I heard the neighbor near my folk's house yelling for his dogs. Apparently, they had found a break in the invisible fence and were frolicking through the neighborhood. The more he yelled, the angrier he sounded, and when I saw the dogs scamper through my folk's front yard they acted oblivious to their screaming pawp.

Judging from the fact that the yelling continued for quite some time, I'm guessing that the dogs did not go rushing back home. Quite honestly, I wasn't at all surprised. If I were one of his dogs I probably wouldn't have raced home either. After all, the dogfather sounded really, really mad and at one point I swore I heard him threaten to unzip someone's fur---whatever that meant.

Let's face it, dogs are not stupid creatures and this whole business of controlling them through domination is an outdated paradigm. Prevailing wisdom suggests that the person who tries to control their dog by using force creates a dog that is fearful and even more difficult to control. In the dog's translation of the human vocabulary, yelling and displays of anger are signs of violence. Bear in mind that among the dog pack, the rest of the group avoids those members that have a violent nature. Cranky pooches are not invited to play by other dogs, and they are certainly not regarded as pack leaders.

When I first heard the deep tone of the neighbor's yelling, I mumbled, "Oh they aren't going to respond to that mean-sounding call." If he really wanted his dogs to consider coming, he should have used a more enthusiastic tone much like the "Who wants a cookie?" way of saying things. At least then the dogs would have known there was nothing to fear and they might have considered coming home out of the desire to show respect to their leader.

The biggest mistake an owner can make is to express anger or extreme dismay when they finally do get their hands on a dog that does not come when it is called. That dog is not likely to forget this negative attitude and is even less likely to come the next time it is called. The logic of this approach becomes clear when you think like a dog: seek pleasure and avoid pain.

Bear in mind that the true dog leader is fair, consistent and behaves according to the situation. This fosters trust and respect. The human leader wanna-be should always use body language to create an environment of respect and engage in practice training sessions that have positive outcomes. In my dog family, I usually integrate informal training sessions with playtime so learning is filled with enthusiastic fun.

I really think the neighbor near my folks could sure use a session of Contemporary Canine Control 101. Though my dogs regularly deposit muddy footprints all over my clothes, it is a rare occasion that they try to walk all over me as their pack leader. – *February 2010*

The Love Junkie

When I was a youngster, our family had a Doberman Pinscher named Orion. He was a sweet and gentle creature that shared a strong bond with my mom. The problem was that when she would leave him, he would do bad things. I remember the time that he chewed a Doberman-sized hole through the family room wall. Once, he removed a set of stairs by gnawing them into a pile of toothpicks. The ultimate destructive act was when he shredded the tires, steel belts and all, of my mother's garaged 1969 MG Midget. If Orion had been a person, my mom might have begged a judge to issue a restraining order.

Many people have shared similar stories about how the love they share with their dog has morphed into Fido's fatal attraction. When left alone, some dogs will stage a home invasion complete with flipped furniture. Others will self-mutilate to the point that they need emergency veterinary attention. In a severe case, one person told me about how his dog hurled itself through a double-paned glass window in an effort to be near his owner while he was walking down the driveway to get the mail.

These are symptoms of separation anxiety. I'm not talking about the pooch that nibbles your slipper because it is bored when you are away. I'm referring to the multitudes of dogs that bark incessantly, heave themselves against the door, or soil and destroy the house when the object of their affection has the foolish audacity to leave home without them. These excessively emotional canines are becoming symbols for the poochie version of the Prozac nation.

In this age of technological proliferation, our face-to-face social interactions have declined. The gathering of friends on Saturday nights is now accomplished over the Internet, and our dogs have shifted to a central focus in our emotional lives. Dogs show us loving devotion that we intensify through elicitation because it feels good to be cared about by another living being. Even with the best intentions, people can create four-legged love junkies without realizing their mistake. These dogs make such a statement when they are left alone that people would rather become prisoners in their own homes than deal with the wrath of their jilted devotee.

In short, dogs that suffer from separation anxiety are overly bonded to one member of their pack. In the single-dog household, the pack member is most likely to be the person that constitutes the dog's "primary" relationship. Loosening the leash strings starts with having your dog spend time bonding with other people. Ask others to spend time walking, feeding and petting your beloved away from your presence.

When you leave the house, be sure to leave a TV or radio playing and give your dog something to keep busy with while you are away. I suggest filling a Kong toy with peanut butter, freezing it, and then tossing it to the dog as you are closing the door with a quick "see ya." Better yet, you might want to consider getting your dog its own four-legged companion. Although you might shudder as you envision double-trouble, it really is a terrific prescription for the dog that suffers from anxiety when left alone. *–February 2007*

What Not to Train

Whenever I give advice about dog training, I am always sure to remind people to be careful about what they train their dogs to do. Sometimes what seems like a good idea at the time can lead to problems down the road. For example, take the new dog owner who gets so excited by hearing the first bark of their puppy that they encourage the pup to "speak" so everyone else can hear the adorable little yarf. This owner shouldn't be surprised when the cute little puppy becomes a not so cute nuisance barker as an adult.

The same goes for the owner who grumbles back at the play-growling puppy during a game of tug of war. This owner is teaching the dog possession aggression and shouldn't be surprised when their adult dog snarls at them if they try to take something out of their dog's mouth. When shaping behavior, owners should always consider how a conditioned response might play out over time.

Surely, it is usually pretty easy to see the potential negative impact of reinforcing behaviors like jumping up on people, barking and even allowing puppies to "mouth" arms or hands. In my experience, however, I have found that with certain dogs even the most innocent and seemingly "good" training can easily become hugely problematic.

I was doing a bit of interior painting a few weeks back, and found myself leaning against the ladder while taking a snack break. Drew, the smartest of my three dogs, was close by in case a morsel of food dropped on the floor. I don't know if it was the paint fumes or the sugar high, but the next thing I knew, I was using my last bite of whoopee pie to teach my dog to climb the four-foot stepladder. Drew loves sweets, and after just a few tries, my brilliant little spaniel was limbering up and down the ladder.

Almost immediately, I knew that I was going to regret what I had just taught my precocious food-driven diva. The next day, she was already using her new coordination skills to scale a 5-foot high bank of dog crates so she could steal her sister's food. On day two, she managed to climb some stacked items in my spare room and then leaped across onto a goody table for an all-she-could-eat buffet of gourmet dog cookies.

By day three, Drew was stringing more trained behaviors together as she used the climb, high-ten, spin combination to steal a bag of treats off the top shelf of the 7 foot high computer desk. When I discovered shreds of the plastic bag, I immediately staged a "dog gone wild" behavioral intervention and began rehabilitative training to prevent a possible dog explosion from over eating.

In retrospect, I think it would have been much more useful instead to have taught Drew to hold the paintbrush in her mouth. At least then she might have been able to help paint the lower half of the room. –*October 2009*

Controlling Your Dog

I have come to the conclusion that no matter how well intentioned the dog owner, people need to learn to control their dogs.

I say this because while walking one of my doggy divas through the city last week, I had an encounter with a rogue Lab that did not respond to the voice commands of her owner. Interestingly, I had observed this same Lab exhibit the same behavior on another occasion and was surprised to see the owner still had not taken steps to properly control her dog.

So there I was, walking my dog along the sidewalk on one of the recent warm afternoons. We were coming to the end of our journey, and my tired pooch was at my left side, just about keeping up to my pace. Two houses ahead, I noticed a woman sitting in a lawn chair while reading the newspaper and I saw a beautiful yellow Lab lounging at her side. As my dog and I moved closer to the reading woman, I began to tighten up on my leash so that my dog had less room to stray along the sidewalk and I had more control of her movement. I didn't want my dog to rudely step into the other dog's yard.

As we began to pass by the house, I heard the woman tell her dog to "stay" while her dog was springing to its feet. By the time the "y" sound had escaped her mouth, the dog was at a full charge across the yard heading straight for us. Luckily, I was quick to act. Even though I was holding a clean-up bag full of poo-poo in my right hand, I still managed to scoop up my dog to safety as I kept walking.

"Don't worry, she's friendly" I heard the woman say as I continued moving ahead. I confess that I imagined whirly birding my bag of poop straight in the foolish woman's direction. Under my breath I uttered, "Friendly or not isn't the point. This woman needs to learn some petiquette." There is a leash law in the city. This means that if your dog does not respond to voice command 10 out of 10 times, it should always be properly restrained. The moment that the Lab placed one paw on the city sidewalk, her owner was in clear violation of the leash law.

Furthermore, just because her dog is friendly does not mean that mine is. People have gotten severely bitten because they were right in the middle of a fight where a leashed dog was protecting the owner from an unrestrained dog. What's more, not all people like dogs, so if your "friendly" dog charges and frightens a person, then that act is tantamount to the human version of assault. The golden rule: Never, ever let your dog approach any person or anyone with a dog without first asking permission from the person.

The irony is that in a culture where people now get sued for giving hugs to other people, some dogs are allowed to stick their noses in private places where they don't belong. In lieu of acting responsibly, the owner gives the excuse, "Don't worry he's friendly." Yes, it would seem he is. *–April 2010*

The Tail Speaks

It is said that the dog is humankind's best friend because it wags its tail instead of its tongue. This is one of my favorite doggy sayings. Aside from the obvious humor and the kibble of truth to this saying, there is really quite a lot to be said about how the dog's tail acts as a communication device.

In fact, communicating with your dog begins with understanding your pooch's body language. Your dog gives you clues as to what it might be thinking or feeling through an interrelated system of body language. The way that Fido carries its tail is one source of information that reveals much about a dog's attitude or mood as well as its temperament and emotional intensity.

Now let me first explain that there is a difference between the physical position of the tail along the dog's body and the way that the dog carries the tail. The physical position is called the "tail set" and it is governed by genetics. This is the part that determines whether a dog's tail is thick and straight like a Labrador or curled over the back like a Pug. In contrast, tail carriage is about how the dog uses or holds the tail and this is where the opportunity for understanding canine communication lies.

When you think about the tail as an indicator or attitude of mood, just remember this saying: as goes the mind of the dog, so does the tail. This means that when the mental mood is up, so is the tail. The tail will wag when the dog is happy and having fun. In contrast, dogs that aren't feeling well or might be feeling down will hang their tails low. This can be seen in curly tailed dogs as a tail held at half-mast or one that is loosely curled.

Tails also give strong clues about a dog's temperament. Dominant dogs often carry their tails rigidly high and might bristle the hair on the tail when they meet a new dog just to convey their status as top dog. Confident dogs are generally relaxed about their tails and carry them more according to mood. In these dogs, the tail may be up or down, wagging or not, depending upon the situation. In contrast, fearful or insecure dogs will clamp their tails tightly against their rumps. You will often see examples of these tails in the waiting room at the vet clinic.

The tail as a gauge of intensity might be seen when a dog at play suddenly stops to concentrate on a bird and the tail is held stiffly straight out at the level of the back or when the pooch is so happy to see you that the tail wags the entire body.

While the tail is not the only part of the dog that acts as a voice, it sure does unravel some of the mystery about what might be going on in the space between the dog's ears at any given moment.

Now if only science could invent some kind of a tail device for people. What married person wouldn't stand in line to buy one of those to give to their spouse? *–July 2010*

Leave It!

"Leave it!" I howled, and waited for the moment of truth as we kept walking. Out of the corner of my eye, I saw the uneaten half of the hamburger drop from her mouth back on to the sidewalk where she found it. In that moment, I felt like a training goddess because it was clear that all of our hard work had paid off.

Without breaking stride, she turned her muzzle upward and gave me her expected "where's my treat" gaze. I reached into my pocket and tossed a reward. As she caught it in mid-air, I couldn't help but think how delightfully absurd it was that my dog just traded half of a discarded hamburger for a pea sized bit of freeze-dried liver. I tossed her a second morsel because I was so impressed with her sacrifice.

I believe that teaching my food motivated King Charles Spaniel to actually "leave" food has been one of my greatest and most difficult accomplishments. Seriously, food is her middle name. I used her love for food to teach her the entire agility course before she was a year old. Food was the magic element for teaching her to climb the A-frame, weave around poles, and dart through closed tunnels. I even used food to teach her to climb a stepladder just in case she should ever find herself needing to rescue a kitten stuck up in a tree.

When she swallowed the ant-covered doughnut in one gulp while walking last fall, I had future visions of my snack-obsessed dog pawing through recycling bins instead of enjoying her daily walk. This was the moment when I realized my food-focused Fido was in need of some impulse control intervention. Thus, I began training the "leave it" command, which is an invaluable skill that any dog can learn.

Here's what you do. Use your dog's food dish to begin training this skill and practice at mealtime. Hold your dog's dish in your hands and begin to place it on the floor. Each time that your dog moves toward the dish as you begin to lower it, immediately stop your motion and return to full height. Repeat this process of trying to set the dish on the floor until your dog figures out that by being still, the dish will continue to move toward the floor.

After a few sessions of the dish making it to the floor without being touched, you can then add on the "leave it" command. Begin by placing the dish on the floor while telling the dog to "leave it." If the dog edges toward the bowl, pick it up. The dog will quickly figure out to leave the bowl until being released to begin eating. Eating, of course, is the reward. Later, you can modify this basic skill by substituting anything you want to be "left alone" and reward the dog with lots of treats for good behavior.

Trust me, this is a skill worth training. You never know when your favorite aunt will have Chinese food from the local all-you-can-eat buffet hidden in her purse. *–May 2008*

Thunder Storm Phobia

When my new puppy made a flying squirrel dive into my lap from across the room after hearing her first claps of thunder two-weeks ago, I thought it might mean big trouble. Even though she is almost a year old, my chicken little had never experienced a fierce New England thunderstorm firsthand. Luckily, I was present when the explosive booms filled the air so I was immediately able to restore her confidence before she completely wrapped herself around my neck like a scarf.

I say I was fortunate to be home when this happened because being there with my quivering canine meant that I had the unique opportunity to modify her behavior before her initial fear response could escalate into a full-blown case of storm phobia. As many owners already know, thunderstorm anxiety is quite common in dogs and researchers at Penn State University report that 15 to 30 percent of pet dogs are affected.

Scientists aren't exactly sure what triggers thunderstorm anxiety in dogs. Some suggest that these fears may be prompted by a combination of factors including changes in barometric pressure, electricity in the air or simply the loud noise of thunder. Frightened dogs may respond by trembling, hiding, panicking, panting excessively and some dogs even refuse to go outside for hours after the storm has passed. The good news is that if your dog suffers from thunderstorm phobia, there are a few behavioral approaches that you can try to help naturally soothe your chattering canine.

I know many owners who have had great success with systematic desensitization using a thunderstorm CD. Basically, the CD should be played very softly for short periods of time while you keep your dog relaxed with sweet talk and calm petting. Over time, you should slowly turn up the volume and begin to play the CD for longer periods until your dog seems unaffected during noise sessions. Be forewarned though, your dog may learn to associate thunderstorms with getting massages and Fido may begin watching the weather channel for the purpose of booking spa appointments when a storm is approaching.

Other people swear by harp music therapy to calm storm fear. It is believed that those certain vibrations of the instrument that are inaudible to humans as well as blended string tones have an extreme calming effect on animals such as dogs, cats, wolves and gorillas. Although it generally takes about 3 minutes of listening for the music to begin to affect the animal, after about 10-20 minutes most will lie resting or may even fall asleep.

A new method for treating thunder anxiety is known as hug therapy. In this case, special body wrappings or a simple snug t-shirt can temper the body's nerve receptors by providing a constant and unchanging level of stimulus that ultimately acts to calm and ground the dog. Truthfully, I'm not sure how well this would work for my quivering bowl of bow-wow Jell-O. She may be desensitized from getting too many hugs already. –*July 2009*

Crate Training

A friend of mine recently contacted me wanting to know my thoughts on crates. Let me give you fair warning: my enthusiasm regarding this topic is like a Greyhound's esteem for chasing rabbits.

Most people are unaware that in the wild, the dog is a den animal. In fact, dogs feel most secure when they are in a space that is protected on three sides. If you aren't convinced about this, take notice of where your dog goes when it wants to hide out on bath day. Popular places are behind a chair or under the bed when a crate is not available. Simply put, dogs can look to their crates like we do our bedrooms, and many owners are not surprised to find their poochies taking a siesta inside their crates even when the door is left open. Forget about those ridiculous dog visor/sunglasses combos that don't stay on anyway; the crate is the modern dog's "must-have" accessory.

The secret to successful crate training is proper placement of the abode. If you are crating during the night, place the crate in the same room where the master sleeps. The Monks of New Skete contend that the closer a dog sleeps to their primary person, the fewer general behavioral problems it will exhibit. Remember, the dog considers isolation to be the worst form of punishment, so placing a crate on another level away from the family is asking for sleepless nights. Be sure that the crate is big enough for your dog to stand up and turn around in. Place some form of bedding at the bottom.

Crate training will limit your dog's visual stimulation and quell mental activity, creating a sounder sleeping environment and promoting a longer night's sleep. It also keeps precocious dogs from finding danger in the form of chewing electrical cords and prevents the trouble that comes from getting into the trash. Dog professionals generally agree that crating is acceptable as long as the dog is not confined for long periods without food, water, or the ability to relieve itself. What's more, watch how much more dog friendly out-of-town relatives become when they find out that your dog is happy in its own portable crate. *–July 2006*

Jumping on People

A friend of mine has a Lab that leaps. To be sure, my friend is not alone in the experience of this potentially annoying behavior. Many dogs have the bad habit of jumping up on people, especially when they enter through the main door of the family home. Watch how dogs greet one another; this is usually achieved by a quick sniff around the head. Subsequently, jumping up on a person is an attempt to sniff their face and can be interpreted as a modification of the instinctive dog-to-dog greeting.

Although this behavior might occasionally be considered a fun and acceptable activity for the right person, it can become problematic with strangers or on those occasions when you are dressed up. As a general rule, I maintain the paw-print motif fabric is only fashionable for little kids and cat people. It is always a good idea to train your dog NOT to greet people by jumping up on them. Appropriate and satisfying greetings between dogs and people can be achieved by using alternate methods.

Here are a few approaches that can be tried to modify a dog's undesirable behavior of jumping on people.

1.) Ignore the dog. While she's hopping, you stand perfectly still. Don't acknowledge her behavior in the slightest way. Don't even make eye contact. Turn around away from her if she persists. When she finally stops jumping, ask her firmly to "sit" and then crouch down to her level to pat and greet her, all the while praising her ladylike behavior.

If she refuses to stop jumping while you are ignoring her, interrupt her behavior by telling her to "sit" and then reward her behavior with lavish praise.

2.) Command the dog. You will need a team effort for this. One person commands the dog to sit in the presence of a second at the door. Both people praise her for sitting and she receives affection only while keeping her tush planted on the floor.

I suggest using this technique every time people come to the door. In severe cases, it may be wise to begin with the dog on a leash in order to keep some control of her in the presence of the second person.

Command your dog to "sit" and "stay" by your side while opening the door or upon the entrance of the second person. Praise your princess copiously for being such a royal subject. This exercise takes a bit of work, but yields wonderful results not only at home but it can also be used while interacting in public areas as well.

3.) Back away from the mugging. When you see your dog in mid-air about to land her paws on you, take a step backwards and say "off." This disrupts the jig, causing the dog to land on the floor, thereby foiling her intended goal and creating momentary confusion. Remember to commend her for having all four feet on the floor. – *July 2006*

Telephone Barking

A woman recently asked me if I had any suggestions about how to stop her dog from barking incessantly every time the telephone rings. She explained that her dog's annoying yipping continues the entire time she holds the receiver to her ear in conversation.

Incidentally, nuisance barking is the number one complaint among dog owners. It is a common problem that can be very difficult to stop once it has started, and barking in one scenario can quickly spread to other situations. Speaking out of turn can easily become a problem because dogs don't buy into the old adage that "they should be seen and not heard." Clearly, some dogs must believe that boring silences like these should be reserved for cats.

In general, different barking situations require specific approaches to modifying the undesirable behavior that are based upon the individual circumstances. In the case of the furry four-legged answering machine that doesn't seem to have an off button, I can prescribe the following course of action.

If your dog barks when the telephone rings, I suggest "setting the dog up" by prearranging a series of incoming telephone calls at predetermined times. You can synchronize watches with a family member or friend and be prepared for an incoming call. You can also use a cellular phone to call yourself at home while you are already there.

The key to this approach is to praise your dog lavishly for being quiet in the two seconds before the telephone rings and for every moment of silence when the dog tries to catch a breath in-between barks. I'm talking about the "goooooood dog!" in your very best happy voice type of praise. The longer the interval that the dog is quiet, the more lavish the praise should become. Be prepared to make a fool of yourself, as the average dog instinctively wants to please, and will soon stop barking when it understands that silence solicits praise.

Try it. A few sessions of positive praise phone-therapy will usually curb even the most frustrating Fido. –*June 2006*

Potty Training

If you are having trouble house training your small dog, you should know that you are not alone. In fact, small and toy dogs have a reputation for being extremely difficult to house break and even those that appear to be doing well can seem to develop toilet training amnesia with the slightest change in environment or schedule.

Sudden drops in temperature, severe rain or snow, and even the onset of daylight savings time can dramatically increase your chances of stepping in a potty present that your little dog has left on the floor for you. Sometimes this happens because little dogs tend to lose focus on why they are outside due to the fact that they are physically sensitive to cold or wet weather conditions.

The good news is that thorough house breaking is possible. I know this because I once had a Lhasa Apso who was so well potty trained that I actually had to bring a small plastic bag filled with the stone material that was outside on the ground of his doggy run back home whenever we traveled. Without the familiar texture of the small pebbles under his feet, he would simply refuse to go to the bathroom.

Granted it took a lot of work and patience, but my dog was so well trained because I was consistent with house breaking habits. You can do this by first making sure that your smaller dog has the opportunity to eliminate outside at regular intervals around the same times every day. Even during the seasonal time change, instead of requiring the little dog with the tiny bladder to adjust to a new hourly schedule all at once, it helps to shift the bathroom breaks to reasonable intervals until the transition is complete.

You should also make sure the designated bathroom area is always the same. Don't walk your dog on grass one week and then expect it to use the back deck or newspapers inside the next. To avoid confusion, the small dog must have consistent and reliable access to the same potty area regardless of the weather or how lazy you feel.

Always praise your dog when it eliminates outside, and don't let the little dog run loose inside the house until the outdoor bathroom business is complete. If your dog doesn't go potty outside, then you should confine it upon coming back inside. You can try putting the dog outside again a short time later. To be sure, even the most stubborn small dog will quickly learn that using the potty outside means the start of the party inside!

If your dog does make a mistake in the house, you should clean it with an enzyme type cleaner and avoid bleach and ammonia cleaners because their ingredients can cause the dog to return to soil the same spot. Even though mistakes sometimes happen, remember that patience, consistency and a sense of humor are vital for the success of a petite pooch potty plan. *–November 2010*

Pack Leadership

If you feel like your dog walks all over you, it could be that you aren't properly behaving like a pack leader. What most humans don't understand is that the pack hierarchy is the blueprint for creating peace and order in the home. Unfortunately, I find that in everyday life, many people mistakenly behave in a manner that allows their pooches to become renegade top dogs without even knowing it.

Believe it or not, a mixed-up pack order can create behavioral dysfunction that includes everything from resource guarding to separation anxiety. The dog that believes that it is in charge will become defiantly disobedient in order to maintain leadership over the human members of the pack. A power struggle ensues when the inconsistent human suddenly insists that they are the head of household.

In order to become a respected pack leader, you must think like a dog. Although dogs have been domesticated and greatly socialized by people, they still rely heavily on their wolfish instincts for creating cooperative order in the group. The fact is that dogs respectfully rely upon their leaders and they will seldom challenge a strong, fair and consistent pack boss.

Dogs follow a simple set of instinctual pack leadership rules that people can easily mimic in daily life. One important rule is that the leader always eats first. This means that you should never feed your dog from the same table while you are eating. When it is time to fill the dog's dish, you should always make sure that the pooch watches you eat something before you place the bowl on the floor.

The leader is always out in front. This means that you should always be first on the scene and first to leave. You can do this by insisting on going up the stairs and through doorways before your dog does. Pushy four-foots can be managed by using simple sit-stay exercises or by being blocked from rushing by their two-legged leader.

The leader acknowledges the rest of the pack on their terms and on their own schedule. This means when you come home after being away, you shouldn't lavish your dog with attention right away. Ignore your dog for 5 full minutes before giving it an initial nonchalant greeting. Play or petting can begin once the serene greeting is completed.

The pack leader always stands tall. This means that you should not allow your dog to put its paws on your shoulders or tolerate it knocking you over. In fact, in a proper pack order, all of the members give the leader plenty of space to move freely.

Sometimes the fur really flies in my fun-filled doghouse. However, as the affirmed leader among my dogs, I can utter one bark that instantly turns my wild kingdom into a peaceable one. – *November 2010*

Balancing the Biscuit

Many people make the silly assumption that because I have a lifetime of knowledge and experience with dogs that my dogs must be well-behaved little darlings. Nothing could be further from the truth, and I'm about to relate a story about how I started managing the bad behavior of one of my little monsters with creative training.

My oldest dog is a food gremlin. Whenever I am within 20 feet of any food related area, she is underfoot and behaving badly. She's pushed jars off the kitchen table hoping they would smash open. She's broken into biscuit boxes that I was certain were out of reach. One time, my 14-inch high fur covered stomach somehow managed to steal a fresh loaf of bread off the counter. She ate the whole loaf before I realized what she had done.

She's such a haunt during dinner that at one point I actually started standing up while I was eating so she wouldn't bother me. My crisis moment came one night when I was snacking in bed while watching TV. I was about to take my first bite of a freshly warmed toaster strudel, when the belly beast jumped me from behind and grabbed the entire tart out of my hand in the second just before I bit down. I looked at my empty paw in disbelief as she ran off with my snack. I knew it was time to launch an intervention.

Instead of punishing my strudel snatcher, I decided to be proactive by teaching her to hold a bone on her nose as a strategy that I could use to keep her focused on her own food instead of mine when whenever I wanted to eat without being disturbed. Her reward for being patient and holding still while I was snacking, of course, was to steal the bone off of her own nose by flipping it, catching it in mid-air and then eating it.

I began by placing a flat biscuit that was just big enough for her to see and feel on the bridge of her nose. I gently held her muzzle steady while telling her to "hold it." At first, I guided her behavior by holding her muzzle still for a few seconds and then I handed her the biscuit as a reward. In a few short sessions, I was able to extend the time she balanced the biscuit, and soon I did not need to steady her muzzle at all.

Next, I taught her to "get it" by first positioning my hands at the sides of her muzzle to help her catch the biscuit as it fell from her nose when I gave the release command. I worked up to removing my hands entirely, and during those early attempts when the biscuit fell on the floor; I quickly grabbed the treat so that she would learn that there was no reward for failing to catch the cookie. Believe me, after 2 or 3 missed attempts she mastered the "get it" skill.

Now, it is amusing to watch her eyes focus on that sole cookie balancing on her nose while I dunk pieces of my own giant cookie in a glass of milk before savoring them, undisturbed. Now that's what I call just desserts. *–September 2010*

Chapter 3: Home Life

"The dog is humankind's best friend because it wags its tail and not its tongue"
-Anonymous

Photo by Tracie Laliberte

For the Love of Dog

Grieving the Loss of a Dog

One of the most difficult aspects of my life with dogs is having to cope with their departure from this life. For many people, losing a canine companion is like the death of a family member. I know that I am not alone when I confide that more than once I have sobbed helplessly over the passing of a pet. After thirty some odd years of dealing with dogs on a daily basis, you might think that saying goodbye would get easier for me. No bones about it, dealing with the paw prints on my soul only seems to get more difficult as I reflect on the finiteness of earthly existence and I continue to question my own place in this tail-chasing universe.

Coping with the death of a dog is often a painful experience that can leave us howling with heartache. Emotions of sadness or loneliness are perfectly natural reactions to this type of loss. Grief can occur in varying degrees and may be quite profound regardless of your age. Unfortunately, the burden of your sorrow may also be compounded by a cultural mindset of biped superiority. "It's only a dog," I've overheard people say in foolish conversation far too many times to count. The truth is that in modern times the family dog has become more than just a fixture that we passively keep in our homes; the dog is an intricate and inextricable part of the story that constitutes our personal history.

Think about the life events that you and your dog share. Has your dog nuzzled you through the tears of a relationship breakup or sat vigil when you have been sick? I wonder how many moves to a new home, weddings, new babies, holidays, divorces and serious illnesses dogs have shared with people. The real question is: How do we begin to cope with the loss of a friend that is so much a part of who we are?

Memorials, burial ceremonies, and crafted books or boxes of commemoration are some simple ways that we can begin to mourn. There are also some wonderful on-line pet memorial cyber sites where you can post a tribute to your departed or talk with other people who are also dealing with loss. Or, you might consider making a tribute your beloved's gifts of unconditional love and non-judgmental acceptance by obtaining an unwanted pet from a shelter or bestowing an act of kindness on an animal or fellow human in need.

Remember, the sorrow is real and everyone deals with it differently. There is no set timetable for healing, nor is there any right way to grieve. Phone your local ASPCA to find a pet bereavement support group or to obtain the name of a counselor if you or someone you know is having trouble dealing with the loss of a four-legged friend. –*September 2006*

The Dog's Sixth Sense

For the past two weekends, I have been taking a course titled "Healing" at the University. This is a very important class for me; what I will learn will be essential material for my dissertation. My classmates have been a mix of nurses, therapists, and social workers, and though I wasn't the only student to arrive with animal fur stuck all over my navy blazer, you can be sure that I was the only representative from the professional field of dog divas in the room.

Healing has been an informative and interesting class. Over the course of the four days, we learned about all sorts of traditional and complementary healing techniques. We talked about healing the mind, the body, and the spirit of the person. Students also had the opportunity to lead the pack in an exploratory discussion about any topic that interests them. Naturally, when it was my turn to bark, the conversation went to the dogs.

Although it didn't stop me, I was a little worried that my classmates would think that I have a squeaky toy for a brain when I decided to address the dog's mysterious sense of "knowing" that seems to be unexplainable by our western science. As I re-told stories that I've heard over the years about the many dogs that refused to leave the sides of their owners who were seriously ill, I saw heads nodding in agreement. When I spoke about the dogs that seemed to just "know" that something was wrong by the way they shadowed their people from room to room during a personal crisis, I saw smiles.

I had a similar response a few weeks back when I was talking to a group at a nearby public library. I was explaining the phenomenon of how dogs know when their owners are coming home.

Biologist Rupert Sheldrake has conducted studies that suggest that dogs are psychically united with their owners by something called "morphic fields." These connections that Sheldrake describes are like invisible elastic bands of energy that can stretch between a pet and a person even over long distances. Morphic fields account for how lost dogs can somehow find their families who have moved across the country. They also may explain how some dogs and their owners seem to share physical ailments or go into hiding the day before a scheduled visit to the vet.

The more I talk with owners about this magical connection, the less I feel a few kibbles short of a bag. *–November 2006*

Being Honored by the Passing of a Dog

My tail wags at the number of people who have shared their stories and contact me with questions after the passing of their four-legged family members. It has become very clear to me that in this respect, the family dog does more than just connect us with the natural world. This creature that is present in our most private moments also compels us to examine the bigger picture of life and sometimes causes us to ask ourselves some of the "difficult" questions about our earthly existence.

A friend of mine shared the circumstances of the passing of her Shih Tzu named Sophie. She told me about the special bond between her adolescent daughter and the small "older" dog that they adopted a few years prior. Her story went on to reveal that the aged dog was diagnosed with cancer, and despite all of their efforts to extend her life under veterinary care, their angel grew weaker every day.

My friend and her daughter went to visit their ailing friend regularly, but it became clear that their beloved was not going to recover. The time had come for a decision to be made about whether or not to prolong the suffering of this fur-wearing friend who had trusted her humans implicitly.

Fortunately, no such decision had to be made. My friend told me that on her final visit with their dog, the pet stood up from her weakened state and began to bark fiercely at the woman before settling back down. Her daughter followed, hugging her pet and was able to tell her "I love you, Sophie" before the little dog peacefully laid down and crossed into the spirit world. My friend and I had a lovely conversation about the implications of all that this story entails. More importantly, the woman was worried about her daughter, who was present when Sophie died.

Here are some words of comfort I sent to the adolescent girl who lost her dear friend:

"Your mom told me the story about what happened with Sophie. I'm sorry that you had to go through that, but Sophie was so lucky to spend her last years and days under your care – in your home – and knowing your love. I'm so happy that you had the opportunity to tell her how much you loved her. I'm sure she already knew; dogs just "know" these kinds of things. I do want to tell you how blessed you are that Sophie chose "you" as her spirit crossed over. It is an honor to be chosen by an animal to witness the end of its life. Sophie's choosing you also tells you how much she loved YOU, and how much comfort and safety you gave her in her last moments. It is awful to lose a pet and I'm sure you miss her so much, but feel some sort of comfort in knowing that she has honored you. Sophie was such a loving and giving soul that I'm sure she'd be happy to know that you have brought a new puppy into your home. Dogs love so unconditionally that surely there is no greater tribute to her than for you to love another creature the way that Sophie loved you. Her spirit and memory will always be with you." *–January 2007*

Obedience School for People

Forget about obedience school for dogs. What we really need is dog training school for people. I came to this conclusion after seeing a young child actually stick out his little person tongue and lick a strange dog on the nose. That's right, the kid licked the dog while the parents just stood there and watched. If this is not a recipe for disaster, I don't know what is.

The Center for Disease Control estimates that there are 4.7 million dog bites reported every year. Approximately 1 in 6 will need medical attention, and 77 percent of all dog bites are to the face. Among children, boys are more likely to get bitten than girls. I believe that many of these dog-bite injuries could be avoided if parents would teach their children to practice good manners around dogs.

Tell kids to never put their face in front of a strange dog. In dog language, putting your face nose-to-nose represents an alpha dog challenge. Many dogs don't take such rudeness lightly and respond by biting first and asking questions later. The same goes for staring at a dog. The cold-stare is also a direct challenge in the dog-eat-dog world of social behavior. People should always be sure to intermittently avert their eyes when having the canine conversation. Teach your kids that it simply isn't polite to stare, not even at the dog.

Always ask permission before petting a dog. People who love dogs seem to think that every dog is friendly; this is a belief that is simply not true. If the dog's owner does say that it is OK, extend your hand palm side up with your fingers curled in so that it looks like a paw. It is always best to allow the dog to sniff your hand before petting. Don't lean over or crowd a dog while petting it. Instead, keep some space between you and the dog. Please people, teach children not to hug a dog like a stuffed animal.

Wide-toothed grins from humans sometimes can be misunderstood as growls by unfamiliar dogs. Try to keep your mouth relaxed when meeting a dog for the first time, and speak in a soft and soothing voice. High-pitched voices and "barking" at dogs trigger the dog's natural prey instinct. Remember, prey-driven behaviors are those that are used for hunting and killing food. A dog's teeth play a natural and important role in this instinct. A general rule for kids should always be "no screaming, no barking."

I think that it is still a miracle that the dog-licking boy didn't become a human chew bone. I like to think that this dog was amazingly well tempered, but perhaps the dog was just as shocked and mortified by such unsophisticated and beastly behavior. I know if I were a domestic dog and some stranger stuck a slurpy tongue on me, I'd definitely end up in the pound. Heck, I'm a socially refined human being and I get growly when somebody parks too close to my car in the grocery store parking lot. *–March 2007*

Bringing Home Puppy

Since we last wagged, I have added four more paws to my pack. After 11 years of alpha dogging my one-pooch household, the time is finally right and I am finally ready to dig into the raising of another pup.

I've been in the sit-stay position about getting another dog for so long because, as you might expect, I don't take dog mothering lightly. In order to be raised correctly, puppies need time and a whole lot of attention; two things I now have in abundance since completing my coursework at the university.

I think that the spring season is the best time of the year to begin integrating a puppy into the New England household. The mild weather makes toilet training easy because more opportunities to potty outside means fewer mistakes on the living room carpet. The correct way to train is to take the pup outside to relieve itself every few hours, and as far as I'm concerned, May conditions make my part in this process a liver snap. Plus, the fertile ground of springtime offers lots of good smells that entice puppies to piddle on the grass.

Socializing is also a breeze in the warmer months. There are many wonderful pet-friendly outdoor spots where a new pup can meet all sorts of people, be exposed to noises, and learn to relax in unfamiliar places. The extra hours of daylight also mean that instead of just being limited to partying in the park on weekends, you and your dog can make weeknight visits to the growing trend of al fresco bistros that now offer doggy watering bowls. Outdoor activity is a wonderful way to release the excessive energy of youth, thus enabling a pup to sleep undisturbed through the night.

Even better is the idea of introducing a new addition into a household where there is already a dog. Many people are nervous about bringing a second dog into the spoiled single-dog home. What they don't realize is that the older dog will mentor the younger one. My bratty 11-year-old little prince, though he honestly still isn't crazy about my new furry accessory, is teaching her the rules of the pack: where and when we go outside, what the feeding routine is, and the importance of using manners around the pack leader.

It normally takes about a month to acclimate any new dog into a household, and so far we are doing just fine. I've learned to put away my shoes, and the new girl has learned not to pull my old fella's tail. He, in turn, is learning about all of the extra attention and treats that I give him as pay-off for putting up with a precocious puppy.

Now I just have to figure out how to tell my husband, who is a soldier in Iraq, that our new edition has claimed his bed pillow as her own. *–May 2007*

Choosing the Right Dog, Part 1

People are forever asking me to decide what breed of dog is best for them. I believe that this is a terrific request only because it indicates that this potential dog owner is open to information and learning about dogs. Unfortunately, this decision is next to impossible for me to make for someone else.

I have a strong appreciation in one way or another for just about every recognized breed, and harbor a deep adoration for the all-American mutt. Still, I know for certain that not every pooch is right for every person, nor is every dog the same. Over the years I have known my share of Pit Bulls in the right home that are crème puffs, and Labradors in the wrong home that should have been named "Lucifer."

Simply put, "What kind of dog should I get?" is a multiple-choice question with as many possible answers as there are breeds of dogs. Even more complex is that the person asking the question is the only one who can possibly determine the correct answer.

As a helpful hound, I am always glad to lend a paw in helping a person to discover the right canine connection. Years ago I used to try answering this question by asking a question in return:

"What breed are you considering?" This approach really wasn't helpful at all. Now, whenever anyone poses this doggy "trick question," I immediately howl out my "Four Paws for Picking the Perfect Pooch" response.

Are you thinking about getting a four-legged friend and wondering which dog is right for you? My advice: Do your research and follow my "four paws" guidelines:

PAW #1: Intrinsic Qualities. You should always consider a breed's history when beginning to narrow your search. Bear in mind that every breed of dog was originally created for a specific purpose. This means that each type has particular characteristics and strong tendencies to do things that are supported by generations of genetic selection.

Looking into the histories of various herding breeds, for example, will explain what drives Australian Cattle Dogs to climb trees or Shetland Sheepdogs to nudge at the ankles of small children. Breed origin also holds the answers as to why the Maltese will stop at nothing to sleep in bed with you and the Golden Retriever walks around the house gently carrying plush toys in its mouth while fiercely wagging its tail.

Intrinsic qualities are traits such as breed intelligence; sensitivity to sight, sound or smell; activity level and emotional capacity. For example, the reason why the Jack Russell Terrier generally exhibits unbridled energy is because it once used to kill rats in speed competitions. Similarly, the Lhasa Apso is wary of strangers because it originated as an indoor palace guard dog.

Breed histories can be fascinating, and making the mental leap from understanding the intrinsic qualities of a particular breed to how these traits might fit into your lifestyle (another paw) is great fun. –*June 2007*

Choosing the Right Dog, Part 2

When we last barked, I started to give advice about how to go about choosing the perfect pooch. I mentioned the first paw of my "four paws" approach that involves looking at the various breeds and researching the history of those dogs that interest you. I explained that the past reveals a lot about the present tendencies of every breed. These are called "intrinsic qualities."

PAW#2: Extrinsic Qualities. These are the ways in which the present has shaped the life of the individual dog thus far. Find out as much as you can about the parents of a potential pup and the manner in which it was reared starting from birth whenever possible. From birth to 7 weeks of age a pup learns how to interact with its pack. From 7-12 weeks, pups learn how to relate to humans. From 12 weeks on, the pup learns independence and how to respond to its social environment. You can be sure that an orphaned pup raised in a one-person household will be distinctly different from a big litter pup that has been raised around children. Similarly, obtaining a dog at 8 months who has never left the house or seen anyone other than the vet may be at risk to develop social issues.

PAW #3: Home-life. You should look carefully at your home and lifestyle to determine which dog traits might integrate best. Is your home very active or serene? Will you have time to spend interacting with a dog that is super-smart but easily bored? Will your dog need to be a bit independent because you work full-time? Do you like to entertain? In this case you should seek an outgoing four-legged party animal rather than a chicken little that hides behind the sofa. Assess your home-life fully, carefully and realistically while considering the best possible traits both for you and for the happiness of the dog.

PAW#4: Preference. The goal is to find a good match for you in your unique situation. It is o.k. to admit that there are things that either you can or won't be willing to tolerate in a new furry companion. Perhaps you can't imagine prancing a Pomeranian around on your Harley, but are willing to accept that your dog is sometimes possessive of his pink squeaky mouse. Maybe you want a dog that you can wash in the sink, or perhaps you'd prefer one that cleans itself by rolling in the wet grass. It may sound crazy, but I know of people who have chosen yellow Labs as opposed to black Labs simply because they didn't want to deal with black dog hair on the beige Berber carpeting.

Take your time in finding the right pooch, and be sure that everyone in the household is willing to participate in the process. Remember that a dog may be a serious commitment, but the right dog-person relationship leaves paw prints on the human soul. *–June 2007*

Back to School

Perhaps you are a proud parent who will be moving your college student into a campus dormitory in the upcoming weeks. Maybe you are feeling anxious about your prized pup leaving the litter, or perhaps you are doing the Snoopy dance because your life will be your own for the first time in nearly two decades! In either case, you probably are having vivid fantasies about how you will fill all of your free time.

What you don't realize is that your whelping box might soon contain a depressed dog. While you are lunching with the ladies and junior is hanging out at the dorm, many dogs will be hounded by the back to school blues. In fact, it is not unusual for the family dog to fall into a funk at the mere sight of those yellow busses that take away their playmates in September.

Ask anyone who has ever lost a dog or a family member, and they will tell you that the surviving dog often shows signs of mourning. It is perfectly normal for a dog to become listless, have a loss of appetite or become less social when there is a change in the pack structure. Remember, the dog considers its humans as a part of its pack, and a child going away to college constitutes such a change.

The intensity of a dog's feelings of loss will vary depending on the individual dog and the type of relationship that they shared with the pack member who is gone. I've had parents tell me that they felt so badly about seeing their dog mope around all day after their child went away to college, that they exchanged their fantasies of freedom for the job of helping their dog through an emotional crisis.

There are ways that you can prepare the family dog for freshman year. The first thing that you can do is to have your college genius spend less time with the dog in the next few weeks. Believe it or not, the worst thing a soon departing student can do is to give the dog more attention than normal.

On moving day, make good-bye's quick. A simple "see ya later" will be much easier for the dog to bear than a perplexing emotional scene. Dogs tend to want to be closer to their humans when they are emotional, and leaving with an emotional outpouring will take a toll on a sensitive furry sibling.

Once the student is away, parents can make changes in the dog's schedule in order to create a new family dynamic. Take some time to go for a brisk morning walk, cuddle in front of the television, or better yet, sign up for a weekly training session at the local Canine University. Adding some fun activities to your dog's routine will help to shift the dog's focus away from the missing part of the pack.

You can expect it to take up to one month for your pooch to adjust to the changes in your doghouse. Once the pack order re-stabilizes, the dog will appear to go back to normal. And the timing will be perfect, because after about a month is when parents begin to really miss their scholars. This is when the caring poke of a soft muzzle can help mom and dad count the days until Thanksgiving break. *–August 2007*

Leadership 101

After 16 months of military service, my husband is expected to return home from Iraq at the end of this week. He is looking forward to coming home, of course, foolishly thinking that he will be returning to his place as the leader of the pack.

Poor man. My bet is that the minute he walks through the door; my new puppy is going to have him wrapped around her little dewclaw. I'll know how severely she has him bampoodled based on how willingly he submits to her claim on his bed pillow. In the upcoming months of having a new person as a guest in her doghouse, I am sure that my puppy Drew is going to evaluate my husband's leadership qualities. Like all dogs, she is going to pay attention to his use of sounds and body language to understand his role in the pack as well as to determine whether or not he should be regarded and respected as leader.

Like so many human-canine relationships that I know, chances are pretty good that Drew will simply trick my husband into thinking that he is in charge. She will have him giving her cookies whenever she wants, she will steal and hide his socks for attention, and she will demand that he take her out to pee, although she intends only to sniff the grass, during the best play of the football game.

For dogs, leadership is a concept that evolves through everyday activity within the pack. Humans have this crazy notion that if they can "alpha" roll their dog, even if this requires violence, then that means that they are the boss. To be sure, this terrorist activity makes an impression on a dog, but is more important to know that in doggy reality a true pack leader gets voluntary shows of the belly from subordinate members of the hierarchy.

Knowing the military's fondness for PowerPoint presentations, I am in the process of putting together a Pack Leadership 101 slideshow to help ease my husband's transition back into our puppy pen. My project will advise him regarding the everyday methods for establishing an elevated position in the dog hierarchy. The slides include suggestions such as consistently making the dog work for treats and rewards by first obeying simple obedience commands. He will learn that he should regularly go through doorways and down stairs before the dog does, since the leader is always out in front of the pack. He will be instructed always to eat his own meals before filling Drew's bowl and to resist giving in to her constant demands for attention,

More importantly, my slide show will portray the doggy model of leadership. Unlike this idea that we humans have that we should be the "boss" based on a form of authority that instills fear, the true dog leader relies on cooperation and thinks in terms of "we" while inspiring trust. I think that when I have finished my slideshow project, I might send a complementary copy to each of the world's political leaders as a model for promoting world peace. *–September 2007*

Barkbusting

A number of years ago, my next-door neighbor owned a dog named "Pete" who unfortunately spent the better part of his time in the backyard. Pete would be sent outside before my neighbor left for work early in the morning, and the boisterous mixed breed would remain in the backyard all day regardless of the weather. Sometimes the dog would be left outside until late evening if my neighbor happened to be out with friends.

Unfortunately for our little neighborhood, Pete was an extremely vocal dog who spent the majority of his time sitting on the back stairs of my neighbor's house barking to be let back in. Whenever he was outside, my neighbor's dog would yap nonstop. Even worse, the more frustrated Pete would get, the louder he would protest.

I mentioned the barking dog to my neighbor on a number of occasions but it did me no good. Day and night, night and day, Pete barked. I thought about getting animal control involved, but like so many other people in my predicament, I didn't want to engage in what might become a vicious dogfight with my neighbor. I resigned myself to tolerate this un-neighborly behavior, and I did what I could to keep myself from going crazy. I wore my Walkman a lot. I studied in my car under the lights of the local grocery store parking lot during exams, and I slept on the sofa a the far side of my house whenever I needed some beauty rest.

I may have ruined my chances of getting into puppy heaven, but I sheepdog-ishly confess that at least once each day, I wished that Pete would find his way to some distant relative's fictitious "farm" in the country; one from which he would never return. Not surprisingly, Pete eventually ended up at the local shelter.

Although I cannot say that I missed him, I must admit that my neighbor's annoying dog taught me to appreciate peace and quiet. Also through my experience with Pete, I came to empathize with every resident in our community who has ever been tortured by nuisance barking.

When my neighbor recently came home with a new pound hound who began woofing almost immediately upon being unleashed into his back yard, I decided to invest in a new-age device that can only be described as electronic aspirin. It's called the "Bark Solver," and for fewer than fifty biscuits, I can stop my neighbor's dog from barking from up to 40 feet away. The unit is specifically designed for outdoor use and it can be mounted and plugged-in, or can run on "D" battery power if no electrical outlet is available.

The "Bark Solver" works by emitting an ultrasonic correction tone to deter barking. It can also be set to produce a tone that is audible to both dogs and humans whenever the dog sounds off. The best part about this gadget is that the cone can be set up to focus the correction in the direction of the problem yapping. Another neat feature is that this training tool can be adjusted according to how loud the bark must be in order to transmit the correction.

Thanks to modern technology, I can look forward to a continued peaceful relationship with my neighbor. *–October 2007*

Puppy Lessons

When my puppy turned a year old last week, I got to thinking about what a fun year it has been for both of us.

For her, it was about being able to make the high jump onto the bed, stealing socks without anybody noticing, and perfecting her cookie-panhandling stare. For me, it was all about learning how to operate my four-legged chewing machine.

We've had quite a few laughs along the way. We've also had a few scares that I can now laugh about. To be sure, my puppy's fixation with tasting, chomping, eating and swallowing A-N-Y-THING has taught me some important lessons to add to the guidebook for proper puppy parenting.

Lesson #1: Keep one eye on the puppy at all times. I knew I was in trouble the first time that I heard my mother ask me if she should call poison control – "again" – after Drew had managed to eat some of the Christmas Cactus that was perched up high, but apparently not high enough, on a window sill. At this point in puppy hood, we had already called the poison emergency center three times in two days while visiting Nana. As far as I know, my mom is still on a first-name basis with the call-center operator, and it wouldn't surprise me if they exchange Christmas cards this year.

Lesson #2: Buy bones no smaller than the size of the puppy's entire head. I remember another time that I saw Drew's tongue turning blue as she was thrashing around on the sofa. Apparently, I had just barely underestimated the appropriate size chewy bone while grossly overestimating her desire to behave like the princess that I supposed her to be. This panicky scene was due to the fact that instead of chewing, she had decided to swallow the bone whole and it was lodged in her throat. I can still feel her needle-like puppy teeth grazing my fingers as I reached into her throat to free the chewy.

Lesson #3: Teach the puppy to "leave it" on command. The one experience that still tickles my funny bone was the time that we were walking downtown and she dove for something on the sidewalk. She swallowed it before I could catch a glimpse of what it was, but the telltale stain of grease and ants on the sidewalk as well as the proximity to the coffee shop led me to believe that the mystery snack was part of a doughnut. I can still see my darling smiling up at me with ants crawling all over her face and I remember still finding little black bugs on her a week later.

Lesson #4: Remove all tags and buy brown puppy beds. At times, picking up poops from my precious little creature was just as amusing. On any given day there was a surprise to be had. Sometimes they were "Made in China," according to a tag that she had swallowed. Sometimes they were pretty colors from the bites that she managed to take out of her steady stream of new puppy beds.

Alas, my beloved's puppy hood has ended. The fun is not over, however. For her first birthday, I decided to get my dog a friend – a puppy that will probably chew on her. –*March 2008*

Colleges Invite Dogs

September can be a very ruff month for dogs. With their two-legged littermates running off to school, many dogs find themselves home alone with lots of free time on their paws. Some dogs spend their days just moping around while others engage in destructive behavior as the result of boredom. To be sure, dog professionals agree that behavior-related complaints always rise as the leaves begin to fall.

Dogs in families that have college students who move away during the school year can be especially lonely. Knowing this, I'm always on the look out for new and interesting ways to ease Phideaux's back to school blues. This year, I've dug up the Bowser of all bones: Get your hound college-bound.

Believe it or not, the number of pet-friendly colleges and universities is steadily growing in the U.S. In fact, some institutions of higher learning already have pet policies that allow small animals to be housed in student dorm rooms. MIT, UCLA and CALTECH allow students to keep cats. The University of Pennsylvania allows hamsters, birds and rabbits.

It would seem that the people who run colleges and universities are smartening up. For years, studies have shown that keeping pets reduces loneliness, decreases depression, and helps people transition more easily through major life changes. What could be more major to a first-year college student than leaving the safety of the whelping box and winding up alone in a crate at an all-breed kennel?

Of course there are many concerns associated with pet keeping on college campuses such as safety, allergies and student responsibility. Schools that do allow pets not only have strict screening procedures, but they also have implemented well-thought out policies for managing potential pet-related problems such as disruption and deep-cleaning costs.

Allowing dogs to room with students is cutting edge. Eckerd College in Florida and Stephens College in Missouri are two schools that successfully house students with their canine companions. Not surprisingly, the open doggy-door strategy is quite popular. The president of student services at Stephens College explains that the new policy is a major attraction for the school and that enrollment has "almost doubled."

So there you have it. My advice to parents who have High School Seniors who may be worried about leaving the puppy playpen next year: Start the Rover College Bound Fund and get a really big doggy bag. –*September 2008*

Getting a Second Dog

I can hardly believe that it has already been six months since I introduced a new puppy into my four-legged family. Thinking back upon the six months of giggles and joy, the decision to get a friend for my needy adolescent dog was easily the best choice that I have ever made for my pack.

Our furry family is living proof that dog experts are right: Adding a second dog helps to quell problematic behavior that is a symptom of the single-hound household. Bringing home a puppy six months ago meant that my high-energy destruct-o-dog would now have a permanent sidekick to provide a steady source of stimulation and entertainment.

My life has become infinitely easier since I brought home the baby. No longer am I required to throw the toy 187 times after dinner. My house plants have stopped being used as tug toys and the few times I have caught the older one standing on the dining room table were evidently to push stuff off to try to get the little one in trouble.

Introducing a second dog into my home has meant that there are no longer attention issues on a daily basis. They now have each other and I have a big part of my life back. On those rare occasions when the dynamic duo does find trouble, it is usually because they are clowning around and something goes terribly wrong.

Last week's incident of fluffy stuff all over the living room was clearly a case of bad luck. I'm sure it wasn't their fault that the head came off of their toy bear and the stuffing sprung out everywhere. I'm sure my darlings were trying to tidy up because when I discovered the mess, they both had big globs of poly-fill stuck to their innocent little faces.

I'm certain that the whole "money" incident last month was also an accident. I can only imagine that they must have been pretending they were Thelma & Louise when they broke into my purse and stole all of the money out of my wallet. Truthfully, I am happy that they didn't decide to try on my new lip gloss, but what my little felons did with the money brings a whole new dimension to "the dog ate it" excuse.

I'm not sure if they were fighting over who was going to get to keep the loot, or if it was a charade about robbery gone bad and they were trying to hide the evidence. All I know is that when I came upon the comedic crime scene, tails were wagging and there were shreds of green confetti all over the floor.

Fortunately, I was able to piece together most of the bills with scotch tape and bring enough of the mutilated money to the bank to get replacements. Bless his dog-loving "now I've heard it all" heart, the teller laughed heartily. Then he shared his own dog story involving an accidental chewing. –*September 2008*

Protecting Dogs from Coyotes

Sometimes I feel like I'm living in the world of Ripley's "Believe it or Not?" While driving to work early one morning last week, I saw a pair of coyotes walking across someone's front lawn. Granted it was a big front lawn that was part of a big yard on an urban street setting that was definitely more country than city-like. Still, as I came upon this sight, I gasped in amazement.

It wasn't seeing these wild animals that surprised me as much as it was seeing them so close to someone's front door. To be sure, coyotes are a growing menace for urban areas because they are overpopulating a rapidly shrinking habitat. Diminishing food supplies is causing them to rummage through garbage receptacles and dine from pet dishes that are left on the back stairs of homes. Unfortunately, these audacious animals pose a tremendous danger to pet owners simply because a hungry coyote preys on small dogs and cats. Coyotes will also work in teams where one will lure a larger dog away from an area so the other hunter can freely attack a defenseless smaller dog.

The best way to protect your dog is to enclose it within secure fencing at all times and keep it indoors during early morning and evening hours. If your dog must go out to take care of business after dark, it should be accompanied by a human adult, and smaller dogs should be leashed.

Coyotes can be kept at bay by securing trash containers and leaving outdoor food bowls empty at night. Another method, as crazy as it sounds, is to mark yard perimeters with urine. I advised a friend of mine who is a breeder to do this last summer when she had a problem with a coyote forcing its way into her fenced-in back-yard several times while her prized female was in heat.

I won't soon forget the look on my friend's face as I handed her and her husband a plastic bowl and instructed them to make a deposit of urine. Knowing better than to ask questions when I was on a problem-solving mission involving dogs, they followed my request and the next day I returned as the pee-pee medicine woman sprinkling urine with a paintbrush at about Great Dane height on all trees and posts around the perimeter of their property. They bow-wowed to the dog diva turned medicine woman when the coyote did not return.

You see, animals mark their territory with urine. This not only lays claim to a particular area, but it also serves as a warning sign for other animals to Keep Out! The higher up the marking is on a tree or post (where the Coyote's nose may still reach), the bigger the animal and the more serious the warning to the wild animal. Human urine, although an unfamiliar scent, works by cuing the coyote that there is a strange, unknown and possibly very dangerous animal lurking about.

Believe it or not, I have also used small amounts of urine mixed with ammonia to keep cats out of my flower garden and as a natural method for discouraging yard-hopping by stray dogs. Believe it or not: An ounce of pee-vention is worth a ton of coyote cure. – *January 2009*

Have an Emergency Plan

I recently learned the value of having a pet crisis contingency plan. In the weeks following Hurricane Katrina, Americans became sadly aware of the consequences associated with pets and people in emergency situations. I always knew having an emergency plan was important, but I never seriously thought that a situation would arise where I would need anything more than the simple strategy I had sketched out in my head.

Seriously, the worry of having to evacuate from my home is not something that has ever kept me awake at night. I always thought that IF ever there were an emergency, I would know what I needed for my animals and exactly where to find it. I felt comfortable in my ability to be level headed under pressure, and I was convinced that surely I'd have fair warning and plenty of time to get ready before a disaster would strike.

I learned a lesson in personal delusion when my doorbell rang in the middle of the night a few weeks ago. The officer standing in my doorway had awakened us at a wee hour to deliver the warning that there was a gas leak in a nearby home and to explain that for safety reasons the gas company was requesting that everyone evacuate right away.

A poll by Zogby International reveals that 61% of pet owners would not leave their residence in an emergency if they could not take their pets with them, and I was no exception. As I calmly closed the door to my home behind me, I had a spaniel slung under each arm. I was quite pleased by the idea that within a few minutes of the ringing doorbell, we were in the car heading toward the safety of a hotel.

I didn't have a clue which local hotels accepted pets, but I remembered that Motel 6 allows dogs and found one listed on my GPS. We were well on our way to security when my thoughts turned to my mental checklist. I started laughing to myself as I realized that I had actually taken the time to dress my dogs in matching sweaters before we left the house, yet I had not taken one single item on my imagined emergency list.

I was completely unprepared. I had no food, water or bowls. I did not grab identification papers or vaccination records. I had no leashes, no toys, and no blankets. I had not even thought to take a toothbrush for myself! Had this been an actual emergency, we would have been in serious trouble. However, to my credit, my dogs looked oh-so-fabulous in their coordinating lavender sequin embellished sweaters!

We ended up having a great adventure at our spaniel slumber party, and when we were allowed to return to our home later the following day, the first thing I did was assemble a pet contingency plan as outlined by the office of US Homeland Security. I now have a disaster survival kit in the hall closet that is stocked with everything that my pets would need in the event of an emergency. It contains all of the items I should have fetched for the gas leak adventure and more. In addition to food and gear, there is a list of local hotels that accept pets, emergency contact numbers, photos of me with my dogs and a pet first-aid kit. And, as you would expect, my doggy survival kit also contains matching "Got Treats?" t-shirts.

–*February 2009*

Home Alone

It's 9:00 am and you are caged at the office for the next eight hours. As you closed the door to leave for work this morning, your dog was melting you with those "please don't leave me" eyes. While you drove to work, you came to terms with leaving your pathetic pooch because after all, someone has to bring home the biscuits. You are at the office and it's 9:02: what do you suppose your dog is doing at this very moment?

Chances are very good that right now your dog is curled up and taking a nice relaxing nap somewhere in your humble abode. It may be on your bed pillow if you have a lot of trust and your dog has a sense of humor, or it may be within the safe confines of a crate if you crave peace of mind. Either way, when your dog awakens from this morning slumber there will be a long day ahead with nothing to do.

Whenever I leave my trio of dogs home alone for any extended period of time, I have learned to provide some boredom-busting activities for them. This helps to keep them from creating their own fun by toilet papering my spare room or trying to fix themselves a sandwich by masterminding the loaf of Wonder bread off the kitchen counter. Mind you, I have small dogs.

One thing that I often do is toss frozen stuffed Kongs or other interactive toys to my darlings to keep them busy while I am gone. Kongs are those beehive shaped rubber toys that have a hollow cavity. You can fill the center with any number of goodies such as peanut butter, packed dog treats or even chicken broth. The trick is to freeze the contents of the toy to make them last longer. For the low-calorie broth treat, you should plug up the small end with a piece of kibble and place the Kong upside down in a coffee mug for filling and freezing.

Sometimes I give my divas long-lasting all-natural tough treats such as bully sticks or swizzles. These are made from muscles, tendons and other disposable parts of food producing swine and cattle. What's best about providing these treats when you are not at home is being able to avoid their highly offensive odor that dogs don't seem to mind. One braided bully stick can entertain my fierce chewer for more than 3 hours.

I also suggest leaving the television on the nature channel or tuning into some soothing classical music on the radio. Both provide some wonderful background noise that helps to mask anxiety-producing sounds that come from outside the house. The television also offers some visual stimulation for those dogs that insist on standing on the back of the sofa and tearing open the curtains so they may bark out the window at passers-by.

Remember: Idle paws are the devil-dogs workshop. Be sure to alternate absentee activities to keep your dog's interest and always be on the lookout for new and creative ways to engage your pooch while you are away from home. The other alternative is to spend your entire day leaving the dog messages to "stop that!" on the answering machine. –*May 2009*

Allergic to Your Dog?

Studies estimate that 10-15% of the population suffers from allergies to pets. Physical reactions in people can range from mild sneezing and a runny nose with congestion to severe allergic reactions and life-threatening asthma attacks. Amazingly enough, in spite of this fact the National Institute of Health reports that 25% of allergy and asthma sufferers still choose to keep pets in their homes.

Interestingly, the presence of dog allergens is fairly common and irritants may be found in many public places even when there is no dog present. Major sources of dog allergens have nothing to do with hair, either. The allergic effect of a dog is due to a primary source of allergens that are present in canine saliva. Secondary allergens are secreted by oil glands and are shed with skin cells in the form of dog dander that gets stuck on the hair.

Creating awareness about human allergies to dogs becomes especially important if you are either hosting a party for the upcoming holiday or if you are allergic and will be attending a social gathering where there may be a dog present.

If you are planning a get-together and you have a dog, you should be mindful of the possibility that one or more of your guests may suffer from allergies to pets. One thing you can do is to give the party area a thorough cleaning before the festivities. A Hepa-filter air purifier used in indoor areas will also minimize allergens exponentially.

While there is no need to shut your dog away from the festivities, it may be helpful to create a dog-free zone at your party; this is a place where guests may go but the dog cannot. It is also best to bathe your dog the day before or better yet, on the morning of your holiday bash. Consider dressing your dog in a doggy t-shirt to further minimize dander dropping. Most people don't know that the shedding of skin and hair increases when dogs are emotionally stimulated.

If you happen to be an unfortunate allergy sufferer, you may find it interesting to know that folks typically are more sensitive to cats than to dogs. If you know that your host or hostess does in fact have a dog, be sure to have a plan for party going. Consider effective measures such as taking some allergy medication before arriving at your destination and bringing your own irritant-free lawn chair to outdoor gatherings. While at the party, limit your interaction with the dog and practice frequent hand washing to keep allergens from transferring from the environment onto your person.

Another little known approach to minimizing pet allergies is to change your own diet. Interestingly, holistic studies have shown that internally eliminating dairy products from a person's diet significantly decreases external allergic reactions to pets. Paws down, this dog lover would much rather eliminate hot fudge sundaes than to ever consider giving up my canine companions to prevent allergies. *–June 2009*

Dignity at the End of Life

Without a doubt, the biggest and most painful predicament facing every dog owner is developing an unselfish awareness about the right time to say goodbye to a beloved friend. I am keenly aware of the heart-tearing angst that tugs at the leash of end of life decisions not just because I have been in this position, but also because I am forever helping people courageously acknowledge the reality of their own animal's suffering.

I have developed personal relationships with lots of people and their dogs that span for many years. Believe it or not, I am deeply affected by the life process of watching a friend's once obnoxious over-active puppy become a serene and delicate senior. I find it excruciatingly painful to watch the trusting senior deteriorate to a state of near helplessness as its master lives in a world of pernicious denial while selfishly refusing to honor the cycle of life.

A few years ago, a very good friend of mine subjected her 16-year-old beagle to monthly surgeries to remove a tumor that kept growing in the back of her dog's throat. In between visits to the operating table, she would force-feed her pet by placing bits of food on the back of her throat to keep her going. For months, her once vivacious dog laid feeble and motionless at death's door on a comforter in the living room.

I clearly understood that my friend was in a tremendous amount of pain over her beloved dog and I offered hugs and a shoulder to cry on. The razor's edge was that I also lost count of the times I tried to show her the reality of her dog's suffering. My friend simply wouldn't hear of it because every tail wag or soft nuzzle gave her hope that the hands of time would miraculously move backward.

I struggled between being a supportive friend and being an advocate against the suffering of animals. Each time I visited my friend, I cried for her pain. Each time I left her house, I cried and howled for the suffering of her dog and I became even more deeply aware of the responsibility of caring that we humans have for our dogs.

I believe that the dog is the most selfless and unconditional of all creatures. I believe that the stoic and noble dog will bravely endure pain and suffering to hang on at any cost, even in death, to serve the needful wishes of its beloved master.

As dog owners, we have the grave responsibility of showing gratitude and honoring our dogs for the gifts they have bestowed upon us over the course of their lives. At the very least, we owe them dignity near the end of life.

I urge all dog owners to see your ageing or ailing dog through its eyes and not your own. Remember that just because your dog does not whimper as he or she struggles to stand up does not necessarily mean there is an absence of pain. *–July 2009*

Let Sleeping Dogs Lie

I opened my eyes the other morning just in time to realize that I was about to fall out of bed. Seriously. The entire left side of my body was hanging off the bed, and my left foot was actually dangling 6 inches above the floor of the 3-foot drop. I saved myself from the tumble by grabbing on to a clump of sheets that were being firmly held down by a pile of sleeping dogs.

As my eyes focused from this rude awakening, I began to wonder how it was that I could possibly have almost fallen out of my queen-sized bed. The answer was clear: my dogs were conspiring to push me off the bed so they could have more cushy stuff to themselves.

After my husband moved out of the dog-house this spring, I began letting all three of my 12 pound not-so-stuffed animals sleep in bed with me. At first I found comfort in knowing that my eldest was curled up on the pillow beside me, keeping one watchful eye and protective ear open as I slept. It was also great having my toes kept warm on those cool nights by the other two dogs sweetly curled up at my feet.

Now it is nearly four months later and all three sleeping dogs sprawl out every which way. When not stretched out, they are vying for pillow privileges. If the free pillow is occupied, my youngest will lounge across my neck, nearly suffocating me, with every intention of stealing my pillow. While I sleep, they'll poke their paws into my back or snore in my ear. In this August heat, they insist on lying right up against me. No doubt, this is with the hope that I will move out of the way so they can extend their gluttonous little legs closer to the fan.

As a dog diva, I know that it is generally a bad idea to let your dog sleep in bed with you. This is because when a dog sleeps in bed, it is able to engage in alpha behavior by pushing people out of the way. Every time I roll over out of the way or give the dog space because I don't want to wake up the sleeping angel, I am acting as a submissive. The fact is, the true alpha dog wouldn't budge. No way. The true alpha would forcefully lean right back against a pushy pack mate.

Dog professionals know that the best place for the dog to sleep is either in a crate or on a bed of its own on the floor beside the master's bed. Interestingly, as much as sleeping in bed can cause problems, so too can banishing the dog to another room. Trainers suggest that the further away from the master's room the dog sleeps, the greater the incidence of behavior problems.

After nearly being pushed onto the floor, I know that I should probably follow prevailing wisdom and crate my dogs by the bed. However, if I did this, then I just wouldn't feel right about wearing my new "sleeps with dogs" t-shirt. *–August 2009*

Fido Fashion

I have a confession to make: right now my dogs are wearing jogging suits. To the stranger who does not know me, my dogs must look like the spoiled surrogate children of an eccentric female singleton. True, they might be a bit spoiled and I am surely ever so slightly eccentric. However, the simple fact is that I have discovered that dressing my dogs provides a practical solution to some common poochie problems.

Fall is upon us here in New England. The arrival of frost-on-the-pumpkin nights means that my three divas, who just spent all of their summer evenings sprawled out on the floor with their muzzles pointed in the direction of the air conditioner, will now insist on taking over the cushy down comforter that I have placed on my bed.

With each plummeting degree of mercury, the further they will want to crawl underneath the comforter, and the more they will refuse to move when the morning alarm clock sounds. The first couple of times this happened in years gone by, I thought it was adorable that my little princesses wanted to stay snugly warm in bed with their noses poking out from underneath the covers while I got ready for a day at the office. The cuteness quickly wore off when their refusal to move caused me to be late for work two days in a row.

When I bought my first pair of doggy pajamas a few years back, I was embarrassed for myself. The first time I put them on my dogs, I was embarrassed for them. I laughed out loud at the thought of having become one of "those" people who dresses their dogs. At first, I kept the fact that my dogs wore pajamas a secret to avoid the humility of seeing people roll their eyes at me. Nevertheless, the truth was that the dogs liked being warm, and right away the mornings were much easier for me because the divas returned to their enthusiastic selves the instant the alarm sounded.

Almost immediately I noticed something else, too. I noticed that while my pack of shedding dogs were wearing clothes, the amount of hair that was being dropped all over the house was much, much less. Instead of falling off the dogs and cascading onto the hardwood floors, loose hairs clumped up within the fancy attire. In defense of doggy fashion: I proclaim that not only do clothes keep my dogs warm, but these goofy outfits also mean less housework for me.

As a canine couture convert, I now let the dogs wear their fido fashion in public. I regularly sniff out doggie boutique bargains, and it has gotten to the point that the woofie wardrobe is almost as big as mine. This makes sense too, because everyone knows that having more clothes means spending less time slaving to the washing machine. Clearly, this leaves more time to plan accessories for the next day's outfits. –*October 2010*

When a Pet Passes

Without a doubt, the most difficult decisions that any pet owner will make have to do with saying "goodbye" to a beloved four-legged family member. Concerned dog owners contact me quite frequently regarding the many aspects of this subject, so I know that it is one that people often grapple with. What makes this subject all the more difficult for any owner is the simple fact that there is no one correct answer that is appropriate for every owner in every situation. Still, when asked for my thoughts about these very difficult questions, I always try to offer some food for thought and end of life issues happen to be among my favorite subjects to write about.

Recently, the owner of a dog named "Peanut" sent me a question wondering if having an owner present during euthanasia would make the process less frightening for the animal. Interestingly enough, a few days prior I had a similar conversation with a fellow dog breeder who was wondering if I thought that her expected emotional outpouring would make those final moments horrible for her pet.

Over a lifetime of working professionally with dogs, there have been many occasions when I have been present at that moment when a dog has crossed to the Rainbow Bridge. In my younger years, the experience haunted me terribly no matter if the circumstances for putting a dog to sleep had to do with poor health or old age. These unsettled feelings evaporated the day I read some Native American lore about honoring the passing spirit. Through this spiritual tradition, I learned about the nobility of being present with animals in their final moments.

This is my advice for any owner who might be struggling with questions about being with their furry friend in its final moments. If you can be with your pet and offer comfort in those moments, you should definitely consider it. Your presence will surely assuage any fear that your dog might be feeling among people and in a place that he or she might only know from a once yearly visit to the veterinarian.

If an owner's emotional outpouring may be overwhelming and intense, I would say that it is quite possible that this might cause an animal unnecessary angst in those last minutes. Remember, the euthanasia process is aimed at being merciful and painless. In this case, a concerned owner might try to have a family member or trusted friend who knows the dog well to be present and to bring peace in those delicate final moments.

One thing I now know for certain is that when it comes time for an animal's passing, being with one's beloved pet as the soul leaves the body is a witnessing of the highest honor. In being with any animal in this capacity, you are respecting the pet's place as well as your own in the circle of life. *–October 2010*

Healed by a Dog

Happy New Year dog lovers! As many of you already know, I become quite nostalgic at the beginning of a new year. I take time to reflect upon the lessons and events of the year that has passed, and I contemplate the adventures that the upcoming year is sure to hold.

In looking back on any year that has gone by, I always learn something valuable about myself that I might not have noticed along the way as I went through the motions of daily life. Last year was no exception, and I'd like to share a personal story about healing. My hope is that it might be a source of inspiration for any dog lover who may be feeling emotionally wounded.

Dogs are bottomless wells of unconditional love and non-judgmental acceptance. To be sure, when my marriage abruptly and unexpectedly ended May of 2009, the furry companions that I had at the time helped me to remain grounded and moving forward until the beginning of 2010. During that ruff time, my dogs were my therapists. They licked my wounds of rejection and wagged away my feelings of betrayal.

By the beginning of 2010, the divorce proceedings were nearly complete and I was hopeful about moving forward with my life. I had a problem, though. I had lost some of my confidence. As silly as it sounds, it really was no joke. Being betrayed, feeling humiliated and realizing after the fact just how manipulated I was during my marriage had caused me to distrust my own judgment in many areas of my life.

In February last year, a good friend of mine asked me if I would be willing to train and show one of her dogs because she was limited by time and energy. My friend told me that her dog Schuman was a very loving animal with beautiful bone structure. She assured me that he had all the makings of a champion except he had one serious problem: he lacked confidence in the show ring.

When my little furry project arrived in early March, I focused my own lack of confidence on trying to build his. I could empathize with this dog because I could imagine how it felt to be secretly scared out of your wits about foolish things like folding chairs and people with bad breath.

I wasn't sure I could help him but I was committed, so we worked together every day. At first it was really difficult for both of us. Sometimes I would lie awake in bed at night and cry, truthfully not knowing if it was for his struggles or mine. Day after day, we put one paw in front of the other and things got better little by little. He learned from me, I learned from him, and by early summer we both were moving past our feelings of uncertainty and inadequacy.

Schuman became a Champion in August and at his last big show before he went home to Virginia in November, I proudly walked him through a crowd of cheering show enthusiasts who called him the "Showman." Reflecting on 2010, my greatest gift came from a broken dog who helped me to feel whole again. – *January 2011*

Chapter 4: The Human Canine Bond

"Dogs are not our whole lives, but they make our lives whole"
-Roger Caras

Photo by Tracie Laliberte

Dogs as Models for the Good Life

Origins of the Human-Canine Bond

It has been said that the dog is humankind's best friend because it wags its tail and not its tongue. In fact, the dog is an animal with which humanity has shared an intimate relationship for over 15,000 years. What's more, it is also the only relationship between people and a domestic animal that did not require that humans conquer the creature in order to domesticate it. Have you ever wondered how it all began with this furry creature that not only wheedles its way into our hearts, but onto our bed-pillows as well?

Although no one is absolutely certain as to exactly how it was that people and dogs became friends, there are a few plausible explanations. The most popular account is what I call the "dog bone" theory. Scientists believe that early in human history, the most dog-like species of wolf might have hung around the outskirts of camps of nomadic human tribes waiting for an occasional discarded bone from dinner to be tossed their way. In exchange, the dogs kept watch and warned of approaching danger while the people slept. Time and again, Fido must have saved a human from being eaten by a bigger animal. I can see the headlines now: "Dog Rescues Meal Ticket."

A second theory is what I call the "he followed me home" explanation. By this account, human children were believed to have ventured into wolfish dog dens to play with the pups. Perhaps the children found the pups irresistible, and occasionally snuck off with one tucked into the folds of their loincloths. Then again, the puppy is one of the only species of animals that will readily follow a human without being coaxed. So, we can also imagine the most precocious of puppies following the children home to the camp and then winning over the hearts of disapproving adults in that way that puppies do.

Another account is what I call "doggy take-out." As a dog lover, this theory wants me to put my tail between my legs and run, but logic forces me to accept it as a possible option. This explanation involves the use of the dog-like wolf as food for primitive people. Hunters might have killed adult females and then brought their orphaned pups back to the camp where they would have been kept alive as a future food-source for the group. The most aggressive of the pups would have been sacrificed first. Gentler pups would have been kept longer until…you know how this story ends. The next thing you know, the dog is sleeping in bed between the two of you, and you dare not move during the night because you do not want to disturb your beloved friend. *–May 2006*

Spending Time Together

I have always believed that we humans can learn a lot from dogs. Whether it is about the joy of living in the moment, the beauty of unconditional love, or the healing power of forgiveness, dogs can teach us much about life. But, can their behavior provide models for interpersonal relationships? Is it time for Fido to tell Dr. Phil to step aside? You decide.

The following is a true story that was told to me about five years ago. It is still one of my favorites. Naturally, I have changed the names to protect the innocent.

A man that I shall call Bob came to me one day to share the story of his beloved female Rottweiler named Fifi. A few years prior to our meeting, Bob had been involved with a person named Sheila, a woman with whom he had lived for five years. A few years into their relationship, the couple had acquired a puppy. The dog was a joint venture that, among other things, was a sort of symbol of the couple's commitment to one another. Unfortunately, within a year after getting Fifi, there was trouble brewing in paradise.

It all began one summer when Bob bought himself a Harley Davidson motorcycle. Each night after work, Bob would rush home to his Harley. He started spending less time with Sheila, and more time riding off into the sunset on his bike. At first, Sheila didn't mind. But the more time that Bob spent away from home, the more Sheila felt abandoned by him. She became angry. The couple began fighting, or rather, Sheila would yell at Bob, and he would take off on his Harley. It was a vicious cycle. Things between the couple got worse until they finally broke up. Bob moved out. He took Fifi with him.

Bob was looking forward to riding his Harley whenever he wanted without having to answer to anyone. The first night he took off, he came home to find that Fifi had shredded toilet paper all over the living room. The second night, he came home to find newspapers shredded. The following night, the same thing happened. Finally, on the fourth night, Fifi had peed and pooped in the middle of the living room carpet. Bob told me that he felt horrible for having left Fifi alone for so long, and that he stopped riding every night. In fact, he now only rode for a few hours in the afternoon on Sundays so that his poor Fifi wouldn't be home alone for very long.

I couldn't help but wonder how things might have turned out differently for Bob and his girlfriend if, instead of yelling, Sheila had shredded toilet paper and peed on the living room rug. Not very lady-like behavior, I know. But hey, it worked for Fifi. *–April 2006*

Accepting Everyone

I learned my greatest lesson in tolerance from my little black furry dog. The year was 1996, and my four-legged professor was just shy of his first birthday. We were enjoying a lovely fall day while window-shopping on the East Side of Providence, RI. My beloved and I were making our way down Thayer Street, weaving amid the crowds of college students and city folks that were out and about on a glorious Saturday afternoon.

We had stopped in front of this charming ceramics store that had some colorfully painted dog bowls in the window. I was so hypnotized by the whimsy of dots and stripes that it was too late when I finally noticed the horror that was almost upon us. I looked up to see a monster lady heading straight for us. She was picking up speed and crouching like a tiger about to leap on its prey while I stood frozen. She had this 1-foot high blue Mohawk that was twirled into spikes. The jutting hair spears ran from just above the center of her forehead all the way around to the nape of her neck.

Her frayed black shirt and miniskirt were held together by some strategically placed safety pins. Speaking of safety pins, she had them through her eye brows, nose, and I could see the ones through her lower lip reflecting off her black gloss lipstick. Even scarier were the outlines of gruesome tattoos that peeked through her torn fishnet stockings. However, what terrified me the most was the collar jutting with six-inch metal spikes that she was wearing around her neck. Being a naïve country girl, I feared that this colorful city character was about to make shish kebob out of my little dog.

In a flash the spike-wearing lady was upon us and it was too late for me to save my furry friend by scooping him into the protective care of my arms. As I braced myself for the blood-curdling yelps that I was certain would come next, you can imagine how shocked I was to discover that the scary lady wasn't a monster at all. I was amazed to see her joyfully rolling around on the sidewalk with my little pet. In turn, he was crawling all over her, wagging his tail furiously and licking her face while, quite unexpectedly, she was howling with laughter. She asked me about my dog and as we talked, I found her to be an amazingly gentle soul with a tender heart.

My wise little pooch taught me that looks can be deceiving. He taught me that if you take the time to look beyond a tackle box of body piercings and spiked dog collars on people, you just might discover a kindred spirit. –*July 2006*

Healing Broken Hearts

The last couple of weeks have been ruff. Two weeks ago today, my father had emergency open-heart surgery after suffering a heart attack. Thanks to the miraculous advancements in modern medicine and some blessings from the big dog in the heavens above, my dad is doing fine and should make a full recovery.

Believe it or not, my father was allowed to leave the hospital less than five days after having his triple by-pass surgery. On discharge day, mom and I arrived with dad's favorite dog-printed bathrobe for him to snuggle into on the trip home. Upon arriving at the hospital, we exchanged the robe for a list of instructions from the doctor that are as long as a Basset Hound from nose to tail.

Dad is instructed to eat a low fat and low salt diet. He is required to have a visiting nurse and a physical therapist make regular calls at his home. There are the dos: He must exercise, take his medicine, check his weight, and make follow-up appointments while he recovers. There are the don'ts: No driving, no work, no stress, no climbing on the roof to hang Christmas lights. Amidst all of these instructions, however, I did notice that there is a vital piece of medical advice that is missing: A doggy a day keeps the doctor away.

Studies have shown that people who spend time with dogs recover faster after suffering heart attacks or having heart surgery than patients who don't. Of course it makes perfect sense that walking a dog provides a fun form of exercise, and the unconditional love helps combat the post-trauma emotional blues. But did you know that spending time stroking a familiar pet helps to lower blood pressure, slows your heart rate, causes your brain to release endorphins and stimulates your immune system? This type of touch interaction, in fact, provides these physiological benefits to both you and your dog.

You might want to keep this in mind now that the holidays are upon us. Petting your dog will soothe your body and mind. Personally, I spend time petting my dog before and after going to the dentist. I also rub his fur before a big test or having to make a presentation to a large crowd. You can be sure that my four-legged therapist will be right by my side if the in-laws come to visit this month, because unlike red wine, he doesn't cause a hangover.

Since coming home last week, my dad has enjoyed his daily dose of pet therapy and I can see him getting stronger every day. My dog is happy, too. Like most grandchildren, he thinks there's nothing better than getting a daily dose of love and cookies from a grandparent. *–December 2006*

Resolutions from Rover

I love ringing in the New Year. For me, New Year's Day is a day of renewal and abundance. I feel energized by the anticipation of all the exciting things that may happen in the upcoming year. I'm big on the New Year's resolution, too. I give my yearly declaration a great deal of thought and consideration. For a deep dog like me, a philosophical promise is sooo much easier and more realistic than, say, giving up sugary snacks or promising to pump iron at the gym.

My New Year's resolution for 2007 is to get in touch with my inner dog. I plan to take lessons from my dog on living my life more fully. My pet is always in a good mood and approaches each moment of every day as an adventure. He knows exactly how to get what he wants without being pushy, and he never ceases to fill a room with smiles and laughter even on the darkest of days. My dog has infinite wisdom. I can say with certainty that underneath those humiliating bow-adorned ponytails that I make him wear, he holds the secrets to living a good life.

In the upcoming year, I will love more unconditionally and show greater non-judgmental acceptance toward myself and toward others. My dog doesn't care if there is lint on the carpet or if I look fat in a dress, and neither should I. He also doesn't care that I sound like a Beagle when I sing in the car; he's right beside me howling in harmony.

I will be more forgiving of myself and of others. From now on, when someone steps on my paw, I will yelp openly and hold my wounded limb in the air while whining for the offender to see. I will then gratefully accept an apology and go back to playing instead of storming off like a mad dog and holding one of those lifelong grudges that we humans are famous for.

I won't always take myself so seriously. My dog isn't afraid to make a complete fool of himself. He wears his dusty rose-colored bows proudly even when people laugh at him. Sometimes he pretends to be startled by his own tail and plays like it is a monster that is chasing him. For Munch, life isn't about ego; life is about running freely (even if it is only around the coffee table) and having fun.

I will be more authentic and I will live in the moment. When my dog is tired he sleeps. When he is happy, he wags his tail. There's never any guesswork about what he is feeling. He chases butterflies, moths, and the occasional gum wrapper all with the same enthusiasm. I know that if my dog were in my shoes, he'd kick them off and walk barefoot in the grass at every opportunity.

If you are stumped for a New Year's resolution that could transform your life, you might want to consider getting in touch with your own inner dog. This resolution cannot fail, since your own dog will provide you with a perfect model and constant reminder throughout the year ahead. Happy New Year dog lovers! –*January 2007*

Have Dog Hair, Will Travel

I went to a fancy party last weekend. Granted, it was a house party, but it was one of those kinds of backyard gatherings where the boats sailing by in the adjacent harbor provided the backdrop for the guests while they were being served tooth-picked treats from silver platters by a white-gloved staff. When I got the invitation, I knew I wouldn't know many people at this lavish affair, but that didn't stop me from planning to go solo. I confess that I did consider asking if I could bring my dog as an escort, but aside from the fact that his tuxedo is still at the cleaners, I learned that the hostess is most unfortunately a cat person. So with dog hair on my dress, I was looking forward to a Saturday night adventure of rubbing noses with strangers.

The party was a fine affair, and I had a howling good time. I met lots of interesting people, and in spite of the fact that there wasn't a wagging tail or a panting tongue to be seen, dogs filled the air. Talk of dogs, that is.

I have always thought of dogs as the great equalizers. Whether a person is a homeless pauper inhabiting the streets, or a royal queen presiding over a vast kingdom, a dog will provide them both with the same unconditional acceptance. Similarly, the topic of dogs can bridge the abyss between two people who seem to have absolutely nothing in common. Put that homeless pauper in a room with the queen and watch what kind of magic happens when they start to talk about their dogs.

Studies have shown that dogs can act as social catalysts. I talked to one person on Saturday night who told me how her once lonely brother-in-law now has more girlfriends than he knows what to do with since he started taking his Bernese mountain dog on his morning jog through the park. Research also suggests that people who are in the presence of dogs appear to be friendlier than those who are not. No matter, I know for certain that when my furry hunk walks me out in public, he attracts more attention from anonymous passersby than Brad Pitt does paparazzi.

When I can't bring my dog, talking about dogs is my next best secret weapon for winning friends and bow-wowing people. Dog talk is a great icebreaker. Usually something as innocent as "Oh my, I've got a dog hair on my dress" is enough to get the yapping going. Before long, the conversation circle grows and people start digging pictures of their dogs out of their wallets or handbags. Incidentally, research shows that among people who carry photos in their wallets, nearly half have pet snapshots.

The next time you feel lost for conversation or find yourself in a roomful of strangers, as I did last weekend, try talking about your dog and see how greyhound fast you become the life of the party. Personally, I never go anywhere without my few strands of backup emergency dog hair. *–April 2007*

The Sighs Have It

Generally, dogs are good at keeping themselves entertained. My dog is really gifted at making every moment quite cosmic. When I think about how he spends his free time, I must conclude that he has the blue ribbon of doggy imaginations.

Most often, my dog passes the day by playing "wild safari" with his squeaky bunny and his stuffed monkey. Sometimes it's "race car driver" as he speeds laps around the coffee table, and then there's the "fashion show" where he cruises the hallway dragging my dirty socks or other unmentionables. He even pauses momentarily on his imaginary runway to show me what he has before doing a perfectly choreographed turn and going back the other way. Basically, give him a gum wrapper and he's entertained for hours.

Unlike we humans who are generally past and future oriented, dogs live fully in the moment. While the moment may seem like a pretty invigorating place to reside for us humans who do it so rarely, living in the eternal moment is not always so thrilling for the dog. Dogs can, in fact, experience boredom. In search of adventure, many bored dogs will often find things to do that ultimately get them in trouble with people. Others engage in compulsive behaviors such as licking their paws until they become raw.

Sometimes, a bored dog will try to rally its human pack members to join in the creation of fun. Take, for example, the dog that bothers you while you are trying to prepare dinner. You know the routine. First, the dog comes over and pokes you with her nose, but you are busy and attempt to ignore the dog. The dog then tries bringing you a tennis ball and she drops the slimy object by the stove. You gently punt it out of the room with your toes, but the dog immediately returns with the ball. You try ignoring her again, but the dog becomes even more of a pest by getting underfoot. Finally you bark at the dog. You point with one finger while your other hand is on your hip, and you growlingly demand that your dog go and find something to do somewhere else!

You feel guilty as your best friend slowly skulks off. The forlorn glance, lowered-head and limp tail are all postures of submission. The dog goes into the other room, circles noisily before thumping down on the floor. She makes certain to end up in a position where she can still see you, and she is positive that you can see her. Then she makes a very loud and exaggerated sigh that is obviously intended for you to hear: "humpffff." The whole scene is a theatrical production.

What is your dog really trying to tell you?

In dog language, the meaning of the sigh is in the eyes. If your dog's eyes are fully open when she sighs, the sound means: "I'm bored, and I give up." But, if her eyes are half closed, the sigh means: "I'm tired and going to take a little rest."

If you do happen to see your dog's eyes wide open during the dramatic sigh, you might consider reorienting your own experience of the world. Widen your sight to the valuable life-lesson that your

150

dog is trying to teach you: The joy of living in the moment. *–April 2007*

The New England "Petriots?"

Super Bowl, shumuperbowl. Really folks, it's not that I have anything against sports; it's just that my life is so busy that the closest I get to any bowl game is the one that I play with my dog to get her to sit and wait for dinner.

But as it happens, I caught part of the Patriots' last playoff game because it was on television when I brought some cold medicine into the living room for my husband. When my sports fan asked me to sit and watch for a minute, I humored him partly because he was sick, and partly because I was suffering from fan guilt.

At first I feigned interest in the game, but after about a minute I couldn't stop watching. I got hooked the moment I realized that the Patriots must be dog people! The more I watched, the more I was certain that there couldn't possibly be a devout cat lover on the team. The truth be told, I buy into the theory that people keep pets as reflections of themselves and their personalities. As far as I could tell, even though our team's star quarterback has a cat's first name (Tom), the name that he shows to the world on the back of his jersey – Brady – has always been a dog name.

My observations of the Patriots on the field told me that this group has a similar social structure to that which exists in the lives of dogs. During the game, I noticed an obvious hierarchy, task cooperation, and a clearly defined leader. Like our players on the football field, if a pack of dogs were hunting game in the wild, one dog would create a diversion, a few others would have the job of surrounding the prey, and the leader would initiate the attack.

Also like the Patriots players, dogs love to rough-and-tumble outdoors no matter how low the mercury in the thermometer may be. I saw a few players actually wearing short-sleeved shirts in that freezing temperature! In an effort to understand such perplexing behavior, my thoughts turned to how my dogs didn't want to come inside from playing in the bitter cold after our last winter snowstorm. This was strong evidence for my dog-people theory.

As I watched those men dive and dart all over the field after the football, it reminded me of the joy that dogs get from chasing balls. Clearly, tennis balls are well known doggy favorites because of their size and shape, but I do know a German Shepherd who carries a deflated football around the backyard. Let me also mention both the players' and poochies' love for pork products. A dog's adoration for pig's ears and hooves is certainly comparable to a player's passion for cradling that oblong pigskin ball.

I haven't watched a Super Bowl since the 1980's, but I'm planning to watch the upcoming Super Bowl so that I can continue my "Petriots" thought experiment. I may be onto something conclusive in my players-are-dog-people theory when the team members start patting each other on the fanny. Who loves butt-scratches more than dogs? *–January 2008*

Lessons in Love

There are all different kinds of love. Romantic love, a mother's love, first love and true love are just a few. When I see people interact with their pooches or watch the way their faces light up when they talk about their furry friends, I have no doubt that "puppy love" is the greatest of all loves.

Those of us who know dogs are no strangers to their endless capacity to give unconditional love. A dog's affection emanates from the core without judgment or expectations. Even when hurt, the big-hearted hound has the infinite ability to forgive the offender whether they be human or otherwise. I often joke that the only reason why dogs and cats can get along is because Fido is willing to put up with and love the cat in spite of those unpredictable doses of clawing meanness that the kitty is known to dish out. The bottom line is that the majority of our cold-nosed canines possess warm hearts that promote world peace.

At the same time, dogs have the magical ability to bring out the best in the people they encounter. History is filled with stories about how the most horrible humans have been softened in the presence of their dogs. This holds true today in the example of the American prison system. Evidence is mounting that suggests that even the most hardened criminals are melted by the dogs they are partnered with in canine-assistance training programs.

For me, I know that the love I feel for my dog is often so intense that it seems as though my heart might burst like a piñata spilling sweets. On my keychain, I carry a photo of my dog wearing a silly red feather boa around her neck. It is my emergency reminder to "lighten up" when the seriousness of life gets too intense. A glimpse of this photo instantly puts a smile on my face and immediately dissipates negativity.

I have come to realize that the reciprocal feelings of love that my dog and I share do not begin and end with our special bond. Through the years, my dogs have taught me an even greater lesson about love. As models for affection, they have taught me to expand my love outwardly in a world where community and fellowship seem to have withered on the vine and have become replaced by buds of violence and hatred.

A lifetime of observing the dog's willingness to love everyone has taught me that sometimes it feels really good to extend a simple "hello" to a stranger. And, the gentle comfort that my dog has offered me in my moments of strife has inspired me to foster worldly love by engaging in random acts of kindness.

Although Valentine's Day is traditionally the day to celebrate those we love most, I challenge all dog lovers to have the heart of a hound every day, and to live a dog's life by offering puppy love to every person they encounter. *–February 2008*

Puppy Kisses

Most people are awakened by the nasty shrill of an alarm clock in the morning. You may be familiar with this scene: A blaring alarm clock is swatted into silence by the robotic-like hand that springs out from the sleeping zombie in the nearby bed. Fortunately, this is not how I experience my mornings. I have an alarm-clock alternative: I usually wake up giggling as my two dogs cover my face with sloppy, wet puppy kisses.

If you are thinking "eeeew, gross!" – stop right there. You may not know this, but getting slobbered by dog spit is a great way to start your morning. Aside from the feelings of euphoria that set the stage for my entire day, I know that canine saliva has healing qualities. That's right, the therapeutic lick of the pooch is not only studied in modern science, but it is also dogumented in human history.

When your grandmother told you "A dog's mouth is cleaner than yours," to some extent she was right. It has been shown that the mouth of a healthy dog with clean teeth contains fewer bacteria than a human mouth. Even more provocative is the 1990 study at the University of California where scientists proved that dog dribble killed E. coli.

This explains why dogs lick their boo-boos.

The early Romans used dogs for healing. Real-life Askelpion temple dogs were instruments of therapy that would diagnose and relieve human suffering. These sacred dogs would lick the afflicted body parts of ailing people who visited their temples. One such location was unearthed in England during World War II, and this ancient temple contained engraved testimonials from people who claimed to have been cured by their visits with dogs.

Medically, cuddling with dogs has been proven to relieve stress, lower blood pressure, and increase brain endorphins. This probably has something to do with the healing power of touch, the oldest of healing modalities. I think it could easily be argued that the affectionate muzzle and caring lick of a dog constitutes curative touch.

In modern times, it has been discovered that healing licks can be about more than love. My friend Priscilla has a Boxer who has found cancer on people. He indicates the location of the malignant cells by sniffing and licking the suspicious area with intense interest. Priscilla's pooch is not the only canine to have this capability. The first recorded detection of malignant melanoma by a dog was documented in 1989. Since then, the cancer-detecting capability of the canine has become of great interest to the medical community.

I'm not suggesting that you should throw away the hand-sanitizer, use Fido to clean scraped knees instead of soap, or fire the family physician. However, I do declare that no one should underestimate the healing magic of getting some loving licks from the family dog. *–June 2008*

Therapy Work

If you have ever considered volunteering with your dog, I have a kibble of advice for you: DO IT. Therapy dog-handler teams are in growing demand. Philanthropic Fidos are needed in a variety of venues that range from visiting assisted living communities to participating in children's reading programs.

I say "paws up" to human-canine team volunteering because after a year of training and preparation, my fur-covered angel and I made our first official visit to a local nursing home. "Rewarding" doesn't even begin to describe our experience. I don't know who was smiling more, the residents or me, but my time spent witnessing my dog interact with this community has tattooed paw prints on my heart. I felt humbled as my darling lovingly extended her muzzle to patient after patient, looking straight at them while they stroked her ears and talked softly to her. One person hugged my tail-wagging partner close to her chest and thanked me profusely for bringing such joy to her day.

The significance of our visit became clear while stopping by this one particular room where there was a resident who had her arms noticeably tucked and folded inside her gown when we entered to have a visit with her roommate. The moment of truth arrived when out of the corner of my eye I saw the woman's hand quietly poke through her sleeves. Her eyes beamed when I asked her if she wanted to pet my dog.

I found much pleasure in these activities, and my greatest gifts came in those subtle moments that might have gone unnoticed by someone else. Each time I heard my dog's name being echoed in the rooms behind us as we migrated down the hallways, I nosed closer to understanding what might have motivated Florence Nightingale.

Volunteering with my therapy dog was exponentially more enjoyable than I had imagined. It felt wonderful to give back to my community while sharing my greatest passion: the love for humankind's best friend.

If you think that your dog may make a good emotional support therapy dog, I encourage you to give it a try. A good first step is to have your dog Canine Good Citizen tested. From there, visit various Web sites for therapy dog organizations to view their evaluation requirements and to determine which group may be right for you.

Registering your dog with a therapy organization is well worth the effort. Not only do these organizations prepare your team for visits, they also provide a list of facilities that are looking for volunteers and offer incident insurance free of charge for their working pet partners. *–October 2008*

The Goodness of Dog People

One of the women in my agility training class has just lost twenty pounds. She says that part of what motivated her weight loss was the desire to be able to run faster so her dog could have more fun speeding around the obstacle course. Another woman in our class told us that after she got her first puppy, she quit her job as a molecular cell biologist and started a completely new career so that she could bring her dog to work.

This is the time of the year that my thoughts usually turn to giving and goodwill. Hence, it is not surprising for me to encounter wonderful stories about the tremendous gifts of self that people give to their dogs. Personally, I remember a time growing up when my mother traded in her snazzy little two-seater sports car for a vehicle that was big enough to transport our dogs to dog shows. As insane as it sounds to me now because we had small dogs, swapping the adorable TR-6 for the beastly Vista Cruiser station wagon for the sake of the dogs seemed like the greatest thing to do at the time.

It seems to me that there's something about the relationship with dogs that brings out qualities of goodwill in people. I've never met a dog person – a true "dog" person – who wasn't willing to extend a paw during a time of need. This may be true of all animal lovers: I cannot say. All I know is that during those ruff times in my own life, it has always been a pack of dog-lovers who helped pull my sled through crisis.

I wonder: are dog people inclined to do good because they learn valuable life lessons about benevolence from watching their dogs? The dog who never leaves the side of an ailing master can teach us about dogged devotion. The dog who wakes the parents of a child having an asthma attack in the middle of the night speaks volumes about showing concern for others. The rescue dog who searches tirelessly during a blizzard for a missing person provides a solid example of work ethic.

I've also entertained the possibility that the "good dog person" is inherently noble to begin with, and naturally keeps the company of dogs due to the laws of attraction. Like attracts like, and these people may see their own goodwill being reflected back at them through their dogs. In this case, choosing the companionship of dogs may be an unconscious act of self-validation that leads to self-love, thus fortifying the desire to do good.

I may never be exactly certain about what constitutes the link between dogs and human decency. All I know is that when I think about how young people are bombarded with messages of selfishness and surrounded by models of moral ineptitude that may shape them into bad boys and girls, I'm inclined to ask Santa to fill their stockings with puppies instead of coal. *–December 2008*

Dating for Dog Lovers

I was talking with a single friend of mine last week and he asked me where I thought he could meet a nice lady who liked dogs. Believe it or not, a woman recently refused a date with him because he has a dog. I was astonished to learn this, and assured my friend that this woman was a fool. As far as I'm concerned, having a dog confers status. Studies have demonstrated that among a list of other wonderful qualities, people who have dogs make better life partners, are more responsible, and have a greater capacity for empathy than people who own other types of pets or have no pets at all.

I made a few obvious suggestions to my lone-wolf friend about going to the dog park, attending training classes, and hanging out in the dog food aisle at the local pet superstore. I also barked about the latest trend in matchmaking for pet-loving singles: on-line dating websites.

I advised my friend that a simple Internet search would provide a host of websites for singles who love pets that he could choose from. I recommended that he look at the different sites to get a feel for the kinds of services they offer. When I did a bit of sniffing around myself, I found out that while some sites charge small membership fees, many of them are completely free. Some will even allow guests to access for limited browsing without registering.

I strayed around one site for the pet lover that is partnered with the reputable match.com, and I even dug up a couple of dot-coms that cater to dog lovers only. I really liked these sites because in addition to personal matchmaking, they offer all kinds of dog-related information from how to find a good veterinarian to where to attend singles events that cater to dog owners. I found one romance site that even offers breeding searches for the owners of unwed pooches who are looking to start a four-legged family!

If you are on the hunt for love, or know someone who is unleashed and looking for puppy love with someone who must adore dogs, I suggest romping around the virtual dog park. Interestingly, a

2005 study by Biz Rate Research found that three out of four women with pets were more likely to date someone who also has pets. The same study found that even among men, the number is still a staggering fifty percent.

If you decide to open an account and create your own profile, you should remember that studies show that people are perceived as being nicer when they are pictured with their dogs. Another kibble of advice: Deborah Wood, the author of "The Dog Lover's Guide to Dating" suggests choosing a mate by using the same criteria you would for choosing a dog. She says that if you like a sassy or high-energy dog, chances are very good that you would enjoy these same qualities in a potential romantic partner. *–February 2009*

Rover and Relationships

Love me, love my dogs: this is my motto. These words to live by become especially important to any singleton who is searching for the perfect life partner.

Even though my field of expertise is in the area of the human-canine bond, I often find myself dishing out personal relationship advice to people with dogs. Dog lovers come to me with all sorts of questions that range from what to do when Rex growls at a potential date to how to stop Princess from doing the wild thing on the leg of a dinner companion.

"Trust your dog," I always advise people who are getting into new relationships. Dogs have a unique sense about people and sometimes they are better judges of character than we are. I also believe that how a new couple handles conflict or an uncomfortable situation involving a dog is like looking into the window of their future together. We don't always want to see it, but I'm convinced that how a potential mate treats our beloved poochie is an indicator of how they will treat us and our loved ones once the magic of new love wears off.

I was recently told the story of the boyfriend who called a kennel looking to have his girlfriend's dog boarded. As the story goes, the boyfriend was quite put out because he never thought he would have to be making such a phone call. Apparently he was dating a woman who had a dog and he openly admitted that he thought the dog was a bother. At his age, he explained, he really didn't want to be tied down by a dog. He also said that he and his girlfriend each had their own houses and on those occasions when she spent evenings at his house, he thought her teacup-sized dog was a complete nuisance as well as a barrier to intimacy.

My initial response to hearing this story was to think that this man needed to find himself a girlfriend without doggie baggage. Even more compelling was my desire to sniff out this girlfriend and give her a few biscuits of advice. Maybe there's a fleas chance that she is reading right now.

To all doggedly devoted girlfriends: if your boyfriend doesn't want the responsibility of a dog, chances are he doesn't want the responsibility that comes with having a real relationship either. Real life is about every day planning, problems and dealing with the unexpected. Having a dog is a microcosm for the bigger responsibilities that come with having children or needing to care for an elderly parent. Furthermore, if your boyfriend is jealous of your love for your dog, you should send him to the pound. Consider adopting a man who knows that if he could win the same affection that you already have for your dog then he'd really have it all. *–June 2009*

Office Mascots

I consider myself to be quite a lucky dog. Even though I work a few different jobs to put biscuits on my table, I am never far away from my dogs because my professional life is dog-friendly by design. Whether I am working at my full-time or part-time day jobs or spending a late night in my home office, my darlings are always within petting distance. To be sure, having my dogs so near as I make my living not only keeps my tail wagging, but their presence also facilitates a more productive and focused work environment.

A recent study by the American Pet Products Manufacturers Association reveals that nearly one in five companies allow their employees to have pets in the workplace. Surveys also suggest that not only do pets help co-workers to get along better and reduce absenteeism, but they also foster a more creative work environment.

Interestingly, a striking 46 million people who bring their dogs to work reported working longer hours.

With mounting evidence that permitting dogs in the workplace is barking up the right tree, it is exciting news that this upcoming June 26th has been declared national "Take Your Dog To Work" day.

If you think your office space might benefit from the presence of a morale boosting bow-wow, you may be able to win over your boss by explaining how the presence of pets significantly improves the relationship between managers and their employees.

Once you do get permission to bring your dog to work on June 26, be sure to follow a few simple rules to make your day successful. A few days prior, prepare by dog proofing the office. Remove poisonous plants and other toxic items such as correction fluid and markers. Hide electrical cords and wires. Also check with your co-workers to find out if anyone has allergies to pets or does not like dogs.

Be sure your dog's vaccinations are up-to-date and give your dog a full grooming the day before. Put together a bag that contains treats, a leash, a water dish and clean-up supplies. If you leave your workspace regularly, also consider bringing a portable kennel to keep your dog safe and comfortable during those times that you may be away from your desk.

Allow your dog to take frequent bathroom breaks and be sure to limit the number and types of treats your co-workers dole out on visiting day. Most importantly, have a contingency plan to take your dog home in the event that your darling has an aversion to the 9-5 grind. Never leave your dog in your vehicle while you work.

If all goes well, "Take Your Dog To Work" day may be the beautiful beginning of an office romance that won't violate company policy. –*June 2009*

My Greatest Gift

The holiday time of year always seems to run by at greyhound fast speed. This year is sure to be no exception now that we are about to plunge nose-first into thinking about holiday giving. I have always thought that it is better to give than to receive, and the thought of choosing the perfect gift brings to mind a recent experience I had with my youngest dog, "BK."

After having a weekend afternoon family dinner get together, I decided to take my four-legged children out for a romp in the back yard at their grandma's house. Selfishly, I was really thinking that if I moved around a bit then I might be able to make room for a second helping of my mom's delicious apple pie. The dogs dashed to and fro around the yard while I envisioned forkfuls of cinnamon-y sweet pie.

From the corner of my eye, I saw my youngest dog slither into the thicket of the tree line at the far end of the yard. When I could no longer see her tail waving in the barren underbrush, I used a recall command to get her attention. As trained, when I called my darling, she immediately exploded forth from the woods and blasted over to me at top speed. I was very pleased with her, and I could see that she was equally as proud of herself as she pranced circles around me.

When I bent down to praise her, I noticed she was holding what was left of a long-since-dead bird in her smiling spaniel mouth. Bye-bye dreams of pie, hello black bird nightmare. Before I could shout for her to drop it, my princess lovingly placed the petrified prize at my feet and then adoringly stared up at me as if to say "a gift for you." Then, before the "ewww gross" escaped my lips, she threw herself on the dried out carcass and began rolling all over the stiffened icky thing with the greatest of joy.

This delightful rolling back and forth over the dead bird was something that is known in dog language as the "roll of contentment." Sometimes dogs do this in the summer grass or when playing with a favorite toy inside the house. The roll of contentment is the dog's way of celebrating the glory of the moment. In an instant, I too was enraptured by this simple expression of joy from the animal perspective.

I laughed a giant laugh when I decided that my dog must have certainly been reveling in her very own version of gift giving. Seeing her with a few feathers stuck in her ears reminded me about how much fun finding the perfect gift can be, and all the joy that I have to look forward to as the holidays approach. I must confess though, I'm still giggling at the ironic twist of my dog-daughter bringing me a present from the very same woods where I used to dig up weeds and give them to my mom as Christmas gifts when I was a wee lass.

Mom if you are reading this, don't worry: I wouldn't dream of re-gifting the bird. *–November 2009*

The Wounded Healer

Early in my doctorate studies at the University, I remember getting into a heated argument with one of my peers about the dog's capacity to feel emotions. My classmate, an otherwise brilliant man, vehemently insisted that dogs were simply dumb animals that did not possess emotional depth.

At the time, I remember trying to prove my case by providing all sorts of examples and scientific evidence to convince my classmate that dogs DO live emotional lives. Never having forgotten this argument, over the years I have become the doggy Jane Goodall of gathering evidence that demonstrates the canine emotional range.

The dog's capacity for empathy is of particular interest to me, as I think that this unique experience of interspecies understanding is what makes dogs excellent for therapy work. In fact, the concept of the "wounded healer" has been, in part, an underlying motivation for using dogs that have recovered from severe burns in therapy work with human burn victims. Similarly, dogs rescued from abusive situations are commonly included within support groups for battered women.

Through my own fact-finding inquiries, I have no doubt that dogs have the ability to know when a human is feeling bad. I've lost count of the number of people who have told me stories of the family dog who did not leave their side during a bout with the flu. I've read tales of dogs who have pulled depressed owners out of bed and I even scrap-booked an article about a German Shepherd that stole a bottle of prescription painkillers from an owner who had intended to commit suicide.

I was recently excited by a new and amazing personal experience with canine empathy after having cut one of my fingers very badly. It was a severe gash that should have gotten sutures, but instead I stupidly opted for three weeks of band-aids. For the first couple of nights I placed my hand way up under my pillow for protection while I slept. It just so happened that at this same time one of my dogs was also healing from a painful cut that had required a vet visit the week before my finger mishap.

On the third night of sleeping with my hand under the pillow, my dog awakened me in the wee hours of the morning as she insistently pawed at the elbow of my hidden hand. She kept up until I finally moved my hand out from under the pillow and showed her my wrapped wound. She licked at the big gauze bandage on my throbbing finger and gave a concerned whimper and then turned to her own bandage and gave a sniff. After acknowledging our shared state, she cuddled beside me and went to sleep.   Now, when I look at the scar, I do not think about the pain. Instead, I think about the emotional healing that came from the empathic nuzzle from my furry friend. *–January 2010*

Kids and Dogs

When I saw my first yellow school bus this week, I couldn't believe that it was already that time of the year again. Naturally, I began thinking about school, kids and my favorite topic: dogs. My thoughts turned to a visit that I made as a guest speaker with my therapy dogs to the children's "Dog University" after school program hosted by the Berkley Community School in Massachusetts this past spring.

The program was designed to teach kids about the exciting world of canines by introducing them to the various pure breeds as well as to dog care and training. For part of each learning session, the teacher invited dog professionals to speak to the kids about the various jobs that dogs do such as therapy, herding and police work.

The nifty thing about this program was that it demonstrated the magical learning potential that occurs when kids are exposed to dog talk in an educational setting. Over and above the learning opportunities that come from making connections between school subjects such as history and science by using topics such as dogs that genuinely interest young learners, educators are also recognizing how the dogs themselves can facilitate the learning process.

In fact, the presence of dogs is becoming increasingly popular in programs that help children overcome developmental, emotional, and learning challenges. The unconditional love and non-judgmental acceptance that dogs offer create a safe space and motivate children to grow emotionally and intellectually. These doggy qualities are the basis for many social programs that have been created to help children learn to read, to provide safety anchors for those with autism, and to offer furry support to kids that are in crisis due to circumstances such as family changes or being bullied in school.

A family dog can be just as fur-rific for the average student, too. Animals teach compassion, model empathy and help children forge strong social bonds with their peers. This became quite clear to me during my visit to the Berkley School when I saw the kids howl to life as they began talking about their dogs. Their stories created common ground and shared experiences for forming new friendships. I also noticed that even the shy children gushed with enthusiasm as they talked about their furry companions.

It is true that a dog might not be right for every family. However, I do find it quite unfortunate when I hear that the parental decision not to obtain a dog is solely rooted in the potential dislike for the work, responsibility or expense. What these parents don't realize is that adding a four-legged family member might really help their child do better in school and in life. Evidence shows that the majority of top Fortune 500 company executives had dogs as children.

I say move over peanut butter and jelly. Kids and dogs are the new combination for a successful school year. *–September 2010*

Chapter 5: The Dog in Society

"The greatest fear dogs know is the fear that you will not come back when you go out the door without them" -Stanley Coren

Photo by Tracie Laliberte

Ruling the Dog Park

Beware the Designer Dog

While my husband was recently home on leave from Iraq, we spent time together doing our favorite things. We, like most Americans, revel in being a part of the in-crowd of style. We lunched at a trendy restaurant, shopped for the hottest fall fashions, and finally hit the bookstore to spy out the latest bestsellers and sip lattes with the rest of the cool people.

By no big surprise at our final stop, I found myself in the dog book aisle carefully balancing a pile of paperback dog treats in my forepaws when I caught sight of a fellow fashionista who was examining a doggy hardcover of her own. With curiosity, I tilted my head sideways so that I could spy the title on the spine of the book she was holding: "Designer Dogs: The Labradoodle." I gasped in horror! This style slave was about to become a fashion victim duped by a street vendor selling cheap knock-offs at Madison Avenue prices!

Buyers beware of this designer dog. The first thing you must know is that technically ALL breeds of dogs are designer dogs. Humankind evolved the domestic dog from the wolf, breeding selectively for specific traits until individual breeds began to emerge. As time progressed in human civilization, the variety of individual dog breeds grew. We owe many of our modern dogs to the genius of the early Christian monks, who bred dogs in solitary sects as they raced to create the best breed for hunting on the pre-industrialized

European countryside. There were also independent dog designers, such as the tax collector Mr. Louis Doberman, who wanted to create a breed that would protect him along bandit ridden collection routes.

There are more than 400 individual and clearly recognizable breeds of dogs in existence worldwide today, and the Labradoodle is not among them. These authentic breeds are ones that have achieved consistency over several generations of pure breeding among members of that same breed. People, this means that if I have a Labrador Retriever and you have a Poodle and we decide to mate them, the offspring are considered a mixed breed or hybrid. In other words, these early generations of Labradoodles are mutts.

Don't get me wrong; I'm a huge fan of the mixed breed. In fact, the all-American mutt is the premier choice for training to assist the hearing impaired. However, over and above the pop culture misuse of words, what makes me growl is this false claim that the Labradoodle doesn't shed, and the insane $2,500.00 price tag that is attached makes me want to bite. A better bang for your high-end dollar is the Portuguese Water Dog or Curly-coated Retriever.

As for those of you who still insist that the Labradoodle is a designer dog, let me suggest that you check out the other designer dogs at the local shelter. You can be really chic and adopt one of them for around 35 bucks. *–October 2006*

Dog Hair Cleans Oils Spills

My New Year's resolution for 2009 is to find new and creative ways to become more environmentally responsible. So, when I decided that I wanted to replace the tattered grooming table that I have been using as a television stand in my bedroom with a real piece of furniture, I thought it might be nice to "reclaim" something from the local second-hand store instead of buying something new. I was happy to put my resolution into practice last week when I brought home a stray rattan desk from the furniture shelter.

As I excitedly began shifting things around my bedroom to make space for my new desk, I discovered dozens of corner dwelling dog hair dust bunnies that had somehow managed to escape my tirade of daily vacuuming. I swear that by the time I finished rearranging the furniture, there were enough fur balls to make a third dog. "Geez, if I could only find a method for reclaiming all of this dog hair, now that'd be something," I mused to myself with resolution resolve.

It isn't that dog hair is bad for the environment. In fact, animal hair is a protein that fully and easily decomposes. Some people use it for fertilizer, some spin it into yarn for knitting and many people offer it to the birds for nest building. True, these are all good ideas, but what I had in mind was to find a use for my future piles of hair that could ultimately heal the environment.

After some sniffing around, I discovered a great cause that makes unique use of discarded dog hair. The Hair Mats Program, founded in 2000, weaves donated hair into mats and makes fur filled nylon booms that are the latest and most efficient method for cleaning up oil spills. One square foot of a woven hair mat can trap one quart of oil in one minute and the booms are excellent for caging oil in waterways.

Basically the woven mats work through a process known as adsorption, whereby the oil sticks to the hair like a magnet. Oil soaked mats can then be removed and placed in special bins where they are safely decomposed by a certain species of worm. Hair mats not only work wonders for emergency oil spills, but they also have everyday uses such as for drip pans during oil changes, leaky cars, pipelines and other machinery.

Apparently clean hair works best, but as long as pet hair isn't filthy dirty and doesn't include any debris or animal waste matter it is perfectly acceptable for donation. Pet businesses are already involved. Now, individual pet owners are encouraged to save fur in a garbage bag lined cardboard box and mail it to the California redemption center.

In 2008, there were 2,600 oil spills that occurred around the world, and many of these accidents had a negative impact on the environment. When I think about all the dog hair that I swept, vacuumed or brushed during the year, I have no doubt that the hair from my two little dogs alone could have probably cleaned up one spill in its entirety. *–January 2009*

Dog Cruelty In Baghdad

I was surfing the Internet when I noticed a headline about the killing of 200 stray dogs in Baghdad, Iraq. Underneath the headline there was a troubling photo of an Iraqi police officer poised with his rifle aimed at a dog that was lying serenely beside a jersey barrier. There was a second and even more disturbing photo of two very young puppies that had been poisoned and were lying dead in the street as pedestrians stepped around them.

As I read the accompanying article, my hackles raised. Apparently, because there are no dog shelters in Baghdad, a growing number of stray dogs are living in the streets. Reports indicate that since Saddam Hussein stopped eradicating the dog population in 2003, the number of homeless hounds roaming the metropolis has grown to over a thousand.

Iraqi officials recently decided to eliminate stray dogs by shooting them with rifles and by feeding them poisoned meat starting in the western half of the city. The canine killing will extend eastwardly in the early months of next year. This plan to exterminate the dogs of Baghdad was initiated because the curs are frightening the residents of the city and thirteen people died from dog bites this past August.

What the article didn't explicitly explain was that it wasn't the dog bites themselves, but rather infectious disease spread by the dog bites that caused the unfortunate deaths of Iraqi citizens. Interestingly, a study conducted here and published in Pediatrics journal explains that the death rate from infectious disease caused by dog bites at home in the U.S. is 18 deaths per year.

Clearly, the dogs in Baghdad may be more of a problem because they are frightening children so much that some kids don't want to attend school. Adults, too, claim they are scared to leave their homes. I agree that if the dogs are terrorizing the city then something needs to be done. I disagree, however, that death by firing squad and poison are the best methods for dealing with this dog problem. I think that such a display of violence against animals steps too close to promoting violence against people. I can only imagine how distressing it must be for children to see the bodies of dead puppies littering their streets.

Granted, I'm not privy to the full extent of the current canine circumstances in Baghdad that might justify the use of bullets and venom to solve issues related to over-population and disease. I do contemplate the possibility, however, that the foundations of peace in Iraq may simply begin with extending humane treatment to all living things. What better precedent could be set for the young generations of Baghdad than to take a non-violent approach to the simple problem of having too many dogs? –December 2008

Voters Should Do Their Research

I have a confession to make. I've been a bad dog. A few weeks ago while attending a doggie show and tell with my youngest poochie, I humorously said something that I fear might have been taken seriously by some unsuspecting onlookers.

It all happened while I was presenting my puppy to a group of novice dog enthusiasts. You see, my furry little friend is at the stage in her development where she has this adorable little clump of hair that stands up and curls like a question mark on the top of her head. When the tuft first appeared two months ago, a friend of mine made up the word "schwadizzle," and that's what I've been laughingly calling it ever since.

So, when I found myself surrounded by a group of curious dog lovers and the question about the tuft of hair came up, I couldn't help but tell the crowd that it was a schwadizzle. The problem was that this dog pack didn't know about my wacky sense of humor and I described my pet's curious feature with a straight face that would make poker players envious. "Oh, that's the schwadizzle" I heard someone repeat with a hint of awe. But, before I could let on about the joke, something interrupted our discussion.

As I drove home that evening, I wondered how many people might have actually believed me about this special canine feature. I began to feel terrible as I imagined them telling their friends about it, or perhaps even Googling to see if they could find other examples of schwadizzles.

Nah, they couldn't REALLY have believed me, could they have?

The schwadizzle debaucle has caused me to think about tomorrow's election and how serious it can be for people to simply accept what they hear at face value. I am a firm believer that just because the source seems credible does not mean that we shouldn't forever question what we are told.

Whenever I teach college, I always encourage my students to ask questions and to think critically about everything they learn. I remind them that it wasn't all that long ago when the world was believed to be flat, and Columbus was thought to be on a suicide mission when he set sail for the New World.

Before you go to the polls tomorrow, be sure to ask questions. Don't accept campaign claims and promises at face value. If you haven't already, and while there is still time, find out as much as you can about the candidates running for office. Do some research about their character and their political platforms and be sure to think carefully before making a decision. Really investigate the ballot questions as well. Read and consider both sides of the argument so that you can make an informed decision.

To be sure, at one time or another in our lives, every one of us has blindly accepted what we have been told. The Tooth Fairy and The Easter Bunny are testament to this. The truth is, however, that tomorrow will be a very important day for the future of all Americans. When you go to the polls, please don't be bamboozled by a schwadizzle. –*November 2008*

Designer Dogs

I wanted to roll over and play dead a few weeks ago when a dear friend of mine asked me if I knew of any breeders of Malti-poos. She explained that she was in the market for a designer dog and told me that she had saved enough money to purchase a really good one.

Immediately, I felt sorry for my friend for having fallen pray to manipulation by the media in this capitalist culture. I explained to her that technically ALL dogs have been designed. People rarely think about it, but the dog is a descendent of the wolf. Humans have technologically engineered the various breeds by selecting for certain traits over generations. As I explained this concept to my friend, I illustrated my point by telling her the story of the tax collector Louis Doberman.

One Louis Doberman engineered his signature breed the Doberman Pinscher in the early 19th century. Mr. Doberman wanted his own personal dog that would protect him from bandits as he traveled the German countryside collecting taxes. He created the breed that we know today by crossing various breeds of local dogs such as the Rottweiler, Greyhound and Manchester Terrier. After breeding for several generations and getting consistent looking offspring, he gifted the world with the beautiful and intelligent dog that is still used for protection today.

When we consider the fact that the purebred dog is the quintessential designer dog, this means that when two purebred dogs such as a Maltese and a Poodle are mated, the Malti-Poo pups that result are considered crossbreeds. When two of those crossbreeds are then bred for consistency over generations until a new breed is formed, only then can we truly call the pups designer dogs.

Unfortunately, the media and some savvy money-minded individuals have hijacked America's love for designer anything and applied it to the business of dogs. I remember there once was a time in the recent past when a Maltese-Poodle mix would simply be given free to a loving home. Now they wear the "designer" misnomer and carry an insultingly hefty price tag. Readers: the people who are selling mixed breed puppies for thousands of dollars are mocking the consumer's intelligence as they laugh all the way to the bank.

Don't get me wrong; I'm a huge fan of the mixed breed. Mixes are the top choice as service dogs for people who are hearing impaired, and some of the most wonderful dogs I have ever known are mutts. However, the intelligent mixed-breed consumer knows better than to spend their hard earned money on fake labels and knows that those thousands of dollars saved can be better used to sponsor hundreds of shelter dogs. –*May 2009*

"Bo" the Presidential Pooch

When I heard the news about the new presidential dog, I began to spin in circles of delight! The first family's choice of an adolescent Portie, in my humble hound dog opinion, really could not have been a more perfectly executed executive decision at a better time.

Although many Americans have been waiting with dog-bone baited breath for the President to make good on his campaign promise to his children, I have been pleased by his reticence about rushing to get a dog. As a responsible dog owner, I understand that getting a new job, moving into a new home AND getting a new puppy all at once is not necessarily the best environment for any dog, never mind one being acquired by a family of first-time owners. Waiting until the family has settled into their new life is the first indication that the Obamas are taking their canine commitment seriously.

After learning a bit about the circumstances of their new addition, I think that Bo is a terrific match for the first family. The Portuguese Water dog is a lively and intelligent breed that is sure to do very well in a high-energy household such as the White House. To be sure, the Obama children will have a loving and hearty companion that will enjoy romping on the lawn by day, and by night, Bo will likely settle in the den with a watchful eye while the kids do their homework.

Acquiring an older puppy is also an excellent choice for this first-time pack family. Although still a goofy puppy, at six months Bo has already outgrown many of the bad habits of puppy-hood like excessive chewing. Even better is the fact that his potty training etiquette is well underway. My earlier nightmares of a young pup gnawing on the legs of the presidential desk after soiling on the rug in the Oval office have now been replaced with sweet visions of practicing sit-stays during important meetings with dignitaries.

It would have been nice to see the President adopt a dog from a shelter, but I really think he made a better choice for his family by going to a breeder and re-homing a returned dog. Breeders are heavily invested in the well being of their dogs and they have background health knowledge about their offspring that just doesn't come with shelter dogs. What's more, by getting Bo from a breeder, the Obamas have done more than just adopt a pet; they've brought home dog years of support from the purebred dog community. This is a network of experts that will help them with any problems they may encounter in their journey as dog owners.

I cannot predict how his term in office will go, but as a potentially responsible dog owner, our President gets two dewclaws up from this pet professional. *–April 2009*

Guide Dogs for the Blind

In 1927, a wealthy American named Dorothy Harris Eustis was breeding show quality German Shepherds in Switzerland. She enjoyed her dogs, but always thought that breeding for beauty did not make the best use of the breed's intelligence, alertness, stamina and sense of responsibility that it seemed to show towards people. While on a trip to Germany, Dorothy visited a school where she saw Shepherds being trained to serve as guides to blind veteran soldiers of World War I. She was so impressed with what she saw that she wrote about it in an article for the *Saturday Evening Post* that same year.

Back in the states, a concerned father from Nashville, Tennessee read the article to his 20-year-old blind son named Morris Frank. The young man had become blind after having two separate accidents that caused him to lose sight in each eye. Unfortunately, back in those days, a blind person was considered to be an invalid with absolutely no hope of living an independent life. As the story goes, young Frank had been deeply disturbed by his choice between either being institutionalized or having to rely upon a full-time caretaker for all aspects of daily living.

Morris Frank was so excited after hearing the article that he sent word to Dorothy asking for her help with obtaining a service dog: "…Thousands of blind persons, like me, abhor being dependent upon others. Help me and I will help them. Train me and I will bring back my dog and show people how a blind man can be absolutely on his own."

Frank courageously went to Switzerland and Eustis helped him. As promised, he returned to spread the word about his gift of independence. This led to the first guide dog school in the nation being founded in Nashville, Tennessee in 1929. The school's first class only had 2 students, but today in the US and Canada there are roughly over 10,000 guide dogs being used by visually impaired individuals.

There are presently 12 accredited schools across the country that train and partner guide dogs with people. Most rely heavily upon private philanthropic donations. This is a noble cause considering the average cost to breed, train and place a dog into the service of one person is estimated to be somewhere around $45,000. No doubt, this expense is priceless when compared to the level of empowerment, independence and well being that the service of a guide dog provides to a human partner over a lifetime.

When Morris Frank died in 1980, he had used 3 service dogs and each was named "Buddy." His dogs guided him along the independent trails of life for over a half-century; this was a rich journey he might not have otherwise known. Today, a life-like full color painted statue of the man and his dog stands in tribute along his once favorite walking path at the Morris Frank Park in Morristown, New Jersey. –*March 2010*

<u>Barking "Jingle Bells"</u>

My dogs have recently acquired a strange new habit. As of late, whenever I am working around the house and turn the stereo on, they abruptly stop whatever they are doing and perch themselves within staring distance of the speakers.

At first I had no idea what was going on, but I quickly realized that they were waiting to hear a song that they love so they could dance and woof along. I think the dogs are convinced that if they stare in the direction of the stereo long enough, they are sure to hear the arfing sounds of their favorite bark-stars come blaring into the living room.

Here's the poop scoop: my doggy divas are shameless groupies of that furry quartet that barks "Jingle Bells." I'm embarrassed to admit it, but I've even caught myself barking along once or twice this season. Although we love this song in my doghouse, the irony is that a New York Times survey of 579 seasonal songs revealed that the barking Jingle Bells was ranked the least favorite holiday song among people.

Don't tell my dogs, but the song was actually created as a sort of joke in 1955 by a man who was quite annoyed by the sounds of barking dogs. The song's creator, Carl Weismann, was actually a renowned ornithologist; this is a person who studies the sounds of birds.

Unfortunately for the Danish scientist, the yaps of barking dogs often interrupted his field recordings of sweet bird melodies. In order to remove these unwanted dog barks from his scientific soundtracks of wild birds, Weismann spliced the hound sounds out by using scissors. The result was a mulching of bark bits on the cutting room floor.

For fun, the clever scientist pieced the barks together to the simple melody of "Jingle Bells" in a medley with a few other nursery rhymes. This project was quite involved, however, as Weismann had to use hundreds of hours of barks in working with the technology of the time in order to fashion the seemingly seamless pitches and tones that became the final recording. The original version also included a carnival barker and was released by RCA Victor here in the US. In 1955, the song sold 500,000 copies.

In 1971, RCA reworked the Jingle Bells segment of the record into a 2-minute holiday single by adding an extra bridge and a full chorus to the track. This is the version that we still hear on the radio today.

I've stuffed the dogs' stockings with an MP3 version of the song and I was able to download Karaoke lyrics from the Internet. I'm only hoping that they won't be too disappointed if Santa Paws doesn't bring them live concert tickets. *–December 2009*

Dog "Devocalization" Bill

The average Massachusetts resident may not know this, but there is a huge legal debate happening on Capitol Hill at this very moment that ultimately affects the lives of every person living in the state. One aspect of the proposed legislation has to do with outlawing animal devocalization. A few readers have contacted me wanting to know more about this practice of debarking dogs.

Devocalization is also known as bark softening, and is a surgical option used to manage the noise output of a dog that is a nuisance barker. The procedure also quells those inappropriately loud or excessively high-pitched barks.

The dog's vocal cords are best described as two small folds of skin in the larynx that open and close to control air and sound flow from the throat. The minor surgical procedure involves either making an incision in the vocal cords or removing a small fold of tissue. Vetz 4 petz explain," The amount of tissue removed from these cases is less involved than that of a tonsillectomy." What's more, side effects from the procedure are minimal.

The term "devocalization" is a misnomer simply for the fact that the dog is still perfectly capable of barking. However, after the surgical procedure, the resulting bark becomes considerably quieter and much less sharply pronounced. The devil-dog's advocate might even argue that true "devocalization," or fundamental removal of a dog's voice, occurs when such a dog is utterly silenced by other alternatives such as wearing no-bark training devices. One might even argue that bark softening IS the humane approach in these cases.

While it is also possible to manage barking through behavior modification and busy tactics, the real-world fact is that even with training some dogs insist on barking incessantly when their owner is not present. In these cases, dogs that live in close quarters such as apartment complexes or those that are excessively annoying to neighbors are typical candidates for bark softening.

As with any proposed legislation, I always remind people to think carefully about the consequences when making laws that limit freedom. A devocalization law would directly affect the dog owner by removing an option that is available to them for maintaining responsible dog ownership. What's more, such a law would also abridge the rights of the non-dog owner. Non-dog owning neighbors may be menaced by a barking dog and might feel forced to chose between moving to a new home or spending their life's savings on a costly legal battle to live a peaceful life. *–November 2009*

Spending Dog Dollars

Looking back, 2009 was the year of the dogfight. Unfortunately, the introduction of dog legislature across the nation relating to animal rights forced dog lovers to choose sides and to battle tooth and toenail in the public forum over proposed laws that seriously threatened our lives with dogs.

On several occasions during this past year, I was asked to support various positions and to make official statements about dog legislature. Sometimes, I was of great help to a particular group. On other occasions, however, I ended up in the doghouse for my refusal to support views that I did not advocate. You see, in my dog's eye view, doing what is best for our canine companions sometimes means having to place trust in people to make the right choices for their own dogs. I firmly believe that each time we bite at the rights of owners to make decisions about their dogs, we nibble away at everyone's rights.

What's more, I believe that the best hope for the betterment of the conditions of dogs in this country truly rests in education and not in passing laws. People need to be taught how to properly relate to dogs. People need to be taught how to properly care for dogs. And, people need to be taught how to act properly and responsibly when their imagined life with dogs doesn't quite turn out as planned.

Quite frankly, I find it abhorrent that humane groups are being lazy by spending money like dog kibble for backing extremist legislation instead of investing the dollars and hours where they are really needed: in the providing for shelter animals. I can only imagine how wisely these same dollars could also have been spent in trying to prevent more dogs from ending up at shelters. When was the last time that you heard of a humane organization offering free obedience classes or sponsoring a program for the public on dog behavior?

To be sure, I would say that the greatest champions for the plight of dogs are the people around us. I was quite enthused to recently learn that my mom, who has an on-line pet boutique, instructed a customer to donate a wrong sized dog jacket that she purchased to a local shelter with a small donation instead of shipping the item back. Apparently, the woman did donate the jacket to the shelter. This angel also added two large bags of pet food, a bunch of toys and a cash donation as well. Before leaving, she placed an ornament on the shelter's holiday tree for "Munch," the name of the dog my mom asked be placed on the jacket donation.

I hope the dog fighting stops in the upcoming year. In my big dog heart, I can dream that extremist humane groups make a resolution to start acting like housedogs instead of alpha dogs and prescribe to spending their biscuits in ways not unlike the "Munch Project."-*December 2009*

Movie Review: "Marley and Me"

Well dog lovers, after its long awaited arrival, the film "Marley & Me" has finally broken out of its crate and run onto the big screen. If you were anything like me, you may have lied to your family about your plans for Christmas dinner in order to sneak out to the movies. My holiday festivities were centered around dining on theater popcorn and M & M's while spending a few hours of laughing and several moments crying during a movie about a terrible yellow Lab.

According to the American Kennel Club, the Labrador Retriever has been the most popular breed in the U.S. for the last 15 years in a row. In fact, in 2004, there were almost three times more Labradors than there were of any other breed registered with the AKC. Its popularity, however, does not mean that raising a Lab is problem-free.

My experience with Labradors made the trials and tribulations of the story of Marley really hit home. In general, the

Labrador is a strongly built, outgoing, and intelligent dog that was originally bred as a retrieving gun dog who would willingly work long hours alongside hunters of birds in very harsh terrains. When not used as a working dog and bored by modern family life, the Labrador's enthusiasm and energy can often work against him.

Labs are born RETREIVERS, which means that they like to hold stuff in their mouths. Unfortunately, with Labs, sometimes this oral fixation goes awry and whatever is in the mouth goes down the hatch. I've heard of Labs swallowing reading glasses, socks, dishcloths and one time a Lab puppy owner told me her precious stole and gulped a fully loaded diaper while master was changing the baby.

Labs are also naturally powerful and extremely friendly; these are two qualities that do not necessarily work well when the dog is tethered to a person or an object. The scenes in the movie where Marley is seen pulling people and towing furniture around were all too familiar to me. I remember once seeing a Lab running down the road with a full length fence post trailing after it. The more noise the post made bouncing off the sidewalk, the faster the dog ran toward the nearest pedestrian.

Marley's serious side in the film does accurately depict how well the breed can thrive as part of the family. Marley's capacity for empathy flourishes when his mistress suffers a miscarriage, and without giving too much of the storyline away, he shows tremendous courage in the aftermath of an assault. I've always maintained that although the Lab is slow to mature, his good character makes him the first to rise to the occasion when called upon during critical times. This is why I believe that Labs make such wonderful and apt service dogs.

At the end of the film, Marley is at last appreciated for the goodness that he has brought to his family. This too, is not surprising. With enough patience and a great sense of humor, any Lab owner will surely discover the wonderful qualities that make the Lab an ideal family dog. *–December 2008*

Pick Up After Your Dog!

Now that the temperature is becoming more agreeable, I have started taking my dog for walks again. We were venturing through the small park behind my house last weekend when I felt something smoosh beneath my sneakers. I looked down and to my horror I saw that we had ventured into a field of doggy land-mine waste. I was so disgusted and upset by this gruesome discovery that I marched right home and returned to the toxic site a few minutes later with my pooper-scooper and a trash bag.

I found this scene so upsetting mostly because I know that it is exactly this problem of not picking up after one's dog that contributes to the general "unwelcoming" attitude toward dogs in our society. I know that the irresponsible actions of one member of the group simply ruin it for the masses of hyper-responsible dog owners.

The concept of responsible dog ownership is also a contributing factor to the recent dog park controversy. As if my opinion matters as much as a single flea on a St. Bernard, I'd like to weigh in on this focus toward "responsible dog ownership."

As citizens of a liberal democracy, we are allowed great individual freedom. With this freedom, however, comes certain responsibilities and moral obligations. As dog owners, we are obligated to keep our dogs vaccinated, healthy, communally quiet, restrained and tame. We are expected not to allow our dogs to menace society; this includes picking up after them, not allowing them to chase kids on bicycles, or scare the mail carrier. These responsibilities seem perfectly reasonable and easy to follow for nearly all dog owners.

The greater mindset of those in power, those people who make and impose the rules of our society, all too frequently supports the reality that the irresponsible actions of a few ruin it for the many. If one person doesn't pick up after their dog, then a NO DOGS ALLOWED sign gets posted. The problem with this mindset is that it is too focused on responsibilities, and as such, flippantly dismisses the fundamental rights of dog owners. Think about it. If a child brings a gun to school and shoots a classmate, we don't put a ban on children going to school. If someone gets behind the wheel of a car and throws trash out of their car window, you won't see a sign on the Interstate the next day that reads, "No cars allowed."

Now I don't pretend to have the answer as to how to instill responsibility in all dog owners, but I know that punishing the whole group for the actions of a few is not within the political design of a liberal democracy. Perhaps the answer lies in requiring the passing of a test or taking a class before licensing a dog. Perhaps the solution rests in imposing punitive fines or the revocation of individual rights of those who act irresponsibly.

For the record, I did pick up that area in the park and I am in the process of building a doggy waste bag dispenser that I plan to place in plain view and keep it filled. I may be living with the prayer for a miracle, but I hope that someday we Americans with dogs can enjoy the same freedom that the Europeans already have: Dogs intermingle with society and are welcome where people are welcome. –*March 2008*

Pet Tax Law Proposal

For me, the arrival of March means sifting through my shoebox full of receipts from the previous year to prepare for filing my taxes. I usually begin by dumping the box on the kitchen table, and then I systematically organize the heap while consuming an entire pot of coffee. Once I've finished, my kitchen table looks like a small-scale Arlington Cemetery with all that remains of money spent neatly piled and lined up according to category.

Of course, the majority of these receipts are worthless when it comes to tax preparation and ultimately they end up in the recycling bin. Nevertheless, this method helps me to identify where I spend my money and it provides me with a financial blueprint.

Did I really say, "blueprint?" After seeing my most recent pile of dog-related receipts that was too thick to staple together, I should say it is more like a financial "pawprint." Unfortunately, even though I consider myself among the AP/Petside poll that shows 50% of the pet owning population considers pets to be family members, I am unable to deduct expenses for my four-footed "children" on my tax forms.

The good news is that this may be changing. In July of 2009, Thaddeus McCotter, a well-intentioned governor from Michigan, proposed a bill that would amend the Federal Tax Code to allow a deduction for pets. The proposed bill, the Humanity and Pets Partnered Through the Years (HAPPY) Act (H.R. 3501), would allow legally pet owning tax-paying individuals to deduct up to $3500 in qualified pet expenses such as food, veterinary and other necessary care on their federal income tax returns.

The bill would not allow the deduction for the cost of purchasing a pet, nor would it apply to animals used for business or in research. However, it would offer some relief in these harsh economic times. Some believe a tax break would encourage responsible pet ownership. It might also cause people to reconsider cost-based decisions for giving up, abandoning or euthanizing pets that need expensive emergency or ongoing medical treatment.

What's more, a tax allowance might provide incentive for people to include pets in their lives. Three decades worth of scientific studies show that companion animals provide many physical, psychological and social benefits to people in all age groups. The fact that pets teach kids about empathy and responsibility or the idea that pets enable aging adults to live longer, healthier and more independent lives should rally support for the bill even among non-pet owners.

Readers and advocates of pet partnerships can support the HAPPY Act (H.R. 3501) by writing or e-mailing their local US Representative and urging them to endorse and co-sponsor the bill. – *March 2010*

Film Review: "Hachi – A Dog's Tale"

Dog lovers, have I got a family movie night rental suggestion for you! Last week, I rented and watched the most wonderful dog story on DVD titled *Hachi—A Dog's Tale*. Starring Richard Gere, the film is about the powerful bond shared between a man and his faithful dog.

Hachi is a modern day adaptation of the true story of the legendary Hachiko, an Akita dog who belonged to a Japanese professor at the University of Tokyo in the 1920's. As the story goes, the loyal Akita ventured over to the Shibuya train station daily to greet his master upon returning home from work. When the professor died of a stroke at the University in 1925, the dog continued his daily vigil of waiting at the train station for his master who never returned for nine years.

In 1934, Hachiko became Japan's national symbol of loyalty and a bronze statue was erected in the dog's honor at one of the five exits of the Shibuya station. The statue is still a well-known and popular meeting spot in Tokyo today. In 1987, a Japanese film was made that told the dog's heroic story. This original film loosely became the basis for the recent Hollywood remake.

The producer of the film Vicki Shigekuni explains that *Hachi* is not just a story about a dog. She suggests that the legendary tale is "a story of universal devotion, and represents any deep bond between a man and woman, parent and child." There is no doubt that Richard Gere and the various dogs who play the canine hero bark this message loudly on the big screen.

Interestingly, Richard Gere read the script several times and found himself crying by the end each time. After deciding to become involved with the project, he immediately began bonding with the dogs in the cast. This was important because the Akita is a very loyal and devoted dog that often has aggression issues with other animals and sometimes does not accept members outside of the immediate family. Not surprisingly, Gere was introduced to each of the dogs slowly over time until he developed close relationships with all of them. The breed's unique spirit of aloofness, which is certainly not suited for all dog owners, is wonderfully portrayed in the film.

Another reason for watching the movie is that it was filmed close to home. The historic Victorian style Woonsocket, Rhode Island train station was one of the settings for the film. Other scenes were filmed at a house in Bristol, RI and in a classroom at the

University of Rhode Island in Kingston. The film's premier screenings at the Woonsocket Stadium Theater included legislators, dignitaries, local people and of course -- dogs.

The brilliant filmmakers collaborated with the American Kennel Club and invited local Akita breeders to host educational "meet the breed" sessions at the premiers where film attendees could learn more about the breed and responsible dog ownership. The hope was that people might think twice before going out and buying an Akita after seeing the film. This was a smart move because, trust me, this is the kind of movie that will make you wish for paw prints on your heart. *–May 2010*

The Canine Partner's Program

I was attending a dog show last weekend when I overhead a spectator ask an exhibitor what kind of dog she was showing in Obedience. "It's a Canhardly," I heard the show enthusiast respond. I smiled to myself because I realized what was about to happen. The woman continued, "We call this breed a Canhardly because you can–hardly tell what it is." Of course, she was referring to her loveable and intelligent yet odd-looking German Shepherd, Collie and Beagle mix.

I've got some great news mixed-breed lovers: AKC events are now allowing cross breeds to compete in some of their performance events at all-breed dog shows. It used to be that these events were for pure-breeds only, but since the beginning of April the AKC has been sponsoring a new program that welcomes mixed breeds into competition. This means that the Heinz variety hound is now eligible to compete for all sorts of AKC titles.

The program is called The Canine Partners Program and it is open to mixed breeds who have registered for listing privileges. The inexpensive registration assigns the pooch an AKC number that allows them to compete in Obedience, Rally and Agility performance events. Competing dogs can earn a variety of impressive titles, ribbons and the same notoriety that purebred dogs have been enjoying for years.

Personally, I've participated in all three types of events and I can say from experience that while Obedience can get pretty dog gone serious, Rally and Agility are fur balls of fun for any level dog and trainer. Rally is a less formal obedience style that involves the precise yet low-impact working through a timed course of basic obedience command stations. In contrast, Agility is a high-speed track of tunnels, jumps and teeter-totters that can best be described as an exhilarating physical thrill for both dog and handler.

Getting involved in performance events usually requires a weekly training commitment between handler and dog to prepare for weekend shows. Besides time, the initial investment is really nothing more than a collar, leash and lots of delicious dog treats. The best part is that at the very least this type of training creates a well-behaved four-legged member of the family while strengthening the bond between people and their furry friends.

Companion events can be a great family activity and the competition at AKC dog shows is even open to kids. Since the dog-show season is upon us, now is the time to get started with your own special type of Canhardly. Within a short few months, you could be ready to run with the big dogs at the local dog shows and prove to all of us pure-breed snobs once and for all that mutts really do rule. – *May 2010*

Pet Health Insurance

Did you hear the one about the dog that swallowed the teriyaki stick? His owner sheepdogishly confessed that it took five surgeries and cost fifteen thousand dollars to get the dog well again. Another woman that I met at a nail salon last summer told me that she paws out five hundred dollars a month on medication for cancer treatment for her seventeen year-old Pit Bull.

These may sound like extreme examples, but truthfully I'm hearing stories of outrageous vet bills because of an unexpected doggy health issue all of the time. A reader recently asked me about pet health insurance, and until recently I wouldn't have even considered giving a second sniff to such a preposterous idea. But, frequent visits to the vet to treat my new pup and the fact that my older dog is now eleven got me thinking. Is it possible to put a dollar amount on how much I love my dogs? Do I love them five hundred dollars worth of emergency vet care? Fifteen hundred dollars? Fifteen thousand?

This isn't an easy question to answer. This week, my little one was rough housing with another pup and sustained an eye injury. It was nothing too terrible, but definitely something that needed a vet's advice. As I wrote my check, I started to think about how many dog toys I could have bought with the money. When I returned home, I began investigating pet health insurance and realized that there are pet healthcare plans that would have already paid for themselves in terms of routine and emergency care.

Doggy medical insurance is a hugely growing trend, and one company has reported revenues that have increased at forty percent annually since 1997 after fifteen straight years of losses. My research revealed that there are a handful of companies that offer a number of different plans from routine care coverage to life threatening illness protection. Plans either offer treatment deductibles or offer a percentage of coverage for veterinary visits. Yearly premiums can vary depending upon the age of your dog, and many of the providers offer multiple pet discounts.

Unfortunately, I found exclusions and caps on every one of the plans. Most don't cover congenital problems such as hip-dysplasia for any breed of dog, and one company even provided a breed-specific listing of health problems that do not qualify for coverage. After making a few phone calls, I found one affordable plan that will help defray the cost of routine shots, dental cleanings, emergency illnesses, heartworm checks, and even flea preventatives. So, I signed up with visions of taking my puppy to training classes with the money that I will save.

Pet health insurance may not be for everyone, but for those of us who love their dogs about one hundred thousand dollars, it might just help us sleep at night. Fancy dog food: $25. Doggy spa treatment: $40. Peace of mind in case my dog decides to swallow a teriyaki stick: Priceless. *–July 2007*

Book Review: "Haint"

There's nothing better in summer than hanging out on the back deck with my dogs, a cool bowl of beverage and a good book. As might be expected, poochie paperbacks are my favorite treat, and I am always on the hunt for a good tale. Recently I chewed through a dog story that would make a puppilicious addition to any dog lover's summer reading list.

Joy Ward's science fiction novel "Haint" is a futuristic story about the fate of the Earthly relationship between humankind and the domestic dog as the Apocalypse rapidly approaches. The story is told from two perspectives; one is that of the female adult human Amanda and the other is that of Haint, her beloved Weimeraner dog.

Ward sets the scene in the not-so-distant future when humanity's mistreatment of the earth has caused a hole in the ozone so severe that it imperils the continued existence of life on the planet. In Ward's future, communities have become created around specific breeds such as Weimeraners. St. Bernards, Airedales, and Border Collies because after the trauma of severe loss of human life from war and disease from an earlier time, the only source of comfort that remains is the relationship that humans have with their dogs.

The novel begins at the start of an ordinary day near the end of the world, but quickly turns into a quest as the heroine embarks on a journey with her dogs and two of her closest human friends to discuss the problem of the dangerously low water levels with the Airedale engineers several communities away. The travelers make a number of stops in dog-oriented communities along the way. They find adventure and the reader learns more about the extra-terrestrial origins of the human-canine relationship.

As the story draws to a close, the humans learn what the dogs already know: they have only days left to live. Soon, a space ship appears to transport the spirits of the dogs back to their planet of origin, and the canine companions must make a choice between leaving the people they have come to love, and remaining to face the harsh end of days by the side of humanity.

Although it is science fiction, Ward explores the continuously evolving real life interconnection between people and dogs within each of the unique dog-designated populations in the story. What's more, this cautionary tale ends on a note of hope, which makes it a fun and interesting read for all ages during the dog days of summer.

You can find Joy Ward's "Haint" at your local bookstore or by ordering it on-line at www.borders.com. If you don't enjoy this book, you can always send it to me so that I can use the pages for paper-training my new puppy. –*July 2007*

Dogs On Board The Titanic

I truly lead a life that has gone to the dogs. No matter where I go, even when I leave my own furry-faced friends at home, somehow dogs and dog stories always seem to sniff me out. My recent fido-free trip to Branson, Missouri was no exception. Although Branson sounds a bit like a stray dog to a pure bred princess such as myself, it is actually an amazing hub that is known for its abundance of live entertainment and museums.

It was while visiting the Titanic museum that I unexpectedly found myself hounded by dogs. You see, upon entering the museum, each patron is handed a passport that contains all sorts of neat information about one of the ship's passengers. My passport was that of Madeline Astor, the teenage bride of the richest man on the ship. As the tour commenced, the first thing I noticed was Francis Millet's quote about some American ladies who "carried tiny dogs." Until that moment, I had no idea that there were dogs on board the Titanic, and what I learned about them was nothing short of amazing.

I shouldn't have been surprised when I learned that my passenger happened to be traveling with her husband and their dog: an Airedale named "Kitty." Apparently, there were 12 dogs of various breeds traveling on board the Titanic, and had the ship not sunk in those early morning hours, there would have been a dog show on board later that day.

The dogs on board Titanic were kept in a kennel area in the third class section of the ship. They were tended to by a number of stewards and were fed by the ship's butcher. Although dogs were not allowed to remain in private cabins overnight, they did spend their days roaming and frolicking on the upper decks with their masters.

The night the ship went down, Colonel John Jacob Astor, the husband of my passenger, was rumored to have gone into third class to free the dogs from their kennels even though going into third class was something that was simply not done by a first class passenger. Another passenger, who was not permitted to take her Great Dane on a lifeboat, had to choose between her dog and safety. Mrs. Isham was found drowned with her arms still wrapped around the neck of her beloved dog two days later.

One furry passenger, a Newfoundland belonging to the first officer of the ship, swam in the icy waters beside a lifeboat for three hours until the rescue ship Carpathia arrived. Rigel barked to alert the rescuers of the lifeboat and then helped lead the weary passengers to safety. A sailor on board the Carpathia adopted the heroic Newfie.

My passenger, Madeline Astor, did survive that horrific night but her husband and their dog did not. It is reported that for the rest of her life she never spoke of Titanic other than to say that the last thing she saw was her husband standing on the ship's deck with his faithful dog by his side. *–August 2009*

Fighting Against Dog Fighting

As a dog lover, my hackles have been raised ever since I first started hearing about the Michael Vick dog fighting case. Since his plea-bargain sentencing of 12 - 18 months, and the imminent threat of his being suspended from the NFL, I have heard a number of people trying to excuse his actions in passing conversation. I try to keep my nose out of it, but when I hear "It's just a sport like any other" and "What's the big deal?" I simply cannot let go of the bone.

The participation of dogs in fighting dates as far back as 2100 B.C. when King Hammurabi used to equip his warriors with huge Mastiff-like dogs. These dogs would hurl themselves at the enemy in an effort to arouse fear and terrify them into retreat. For many centuries later in history, dogs were used to help humans hunt dangerous game such as wild boars and bears. These dogs would corner and keep the game at bay while the hunters killed the dangerous animal with a hunting knife.

Dog-on-animal and dog-on-dog fighting in pits gained popularity as entertainment in the English Royal Court in the late sixteenth century. However, by 1835 Parliament passed a law that prohibited any type of fighting between four-legged adversaries, siding with public opinion that dog fighting was cruel and savage.

As an activity that has its roots as a form of "entertainment" I would have to say that such forms of amusement are unfit for a civilized society. Not that I approve of either one, but dog fighting cannot be compared to a "sport" such as deer hunting for the simple fact that a brutal dog fight can go on for as long as five hours. Compared with the single skilled shot of the hunter, the dog dies a slow and torturous death in the pit.

Dog fighting is also a sad reflection of the pernicious violence that pervades our culture today. What kind of message are we sending to our youth and to the rest of the world when we betray those creatures whose care we have been entrusted with?

The fact that Mr. Vick was personally involved with dog fighting activity is bad enough. However, those who stand in his defense seem to be missing the most socially dangerous part of his actions: The fact that he destroyed dogs by electrocution, beating, hanging and drowning.

There is a dog pile of evidence that supports the link between animal cruelty and social violence. Studies have determined that 75% of prison inmates convicted of violent offences have also engaged in cruel behavior towards animals. Animal abuse and domestic violence go paw-in-paw, and children who are cruel to animals have a greater chance of committing violent acts against people as adults.

In short, violent treatment towards animals is a pathway to violence against people. To learn more about the link between violence and animal abuse, visit www.latham.org. -*August 2007*

Thoughts on Dog Food

The recent news of the pet food recall has caused the fur to fly in the lives of dog owners. The day the news broke, my e-mail box filled up with close to a hundred links to the same story from different readers and concerned friends. Even if this mass recall did not affect people directly, it certainly did cause many dog owners to give thought to what they feed their four-legged family members. Since the start of the pet food panic, a number of people have contacted me wondering if I would spill the bones about dog food.

Up until the late 1800's, when the first commercial dog food was invented, dogs basically ate whatever their owners ate. Dogs in various cultures around the world shared the cultural cuisine indigenous to their owners' native lands and traditions. Inuit dogs ate fish and whale blubber. Greyhounds ate rabbit. English herding dogs ate mutton and potatoes. Dogs gratefully dined on the scraps of what was both convenient and available to their human counterparts.

British butchers are credited with introducing the first food intended solely for dogs by packing and selling the leftover scrap meat from the horses that died while working in the streets in London. Kibble was invented in 1870 and was widely available in the U.S. by 1930, but didn't catch on in American until after World War II. Women, who strongly desired every convenience that was available in the post war society, are credited with facilitating what has become the multibillion-dollar pet food industry.

The modern market is rich with choices for nearly every palate. Food can be found in a variety of flavors for dogs of every age. You will see canned, dry, semi-moist, raw, frozen and foil-pouched on the doggy take-out menu. It is also available at nearly every price level from yard dog economical to re-mortgage-the-doghouse gourmet. However, no matter what your hungry dog's indiscriminate palate tells you, when it comes to choosing canine cuisine, you get what you pay for.

Don't be tricked by expensive advertising campaigns and do your homework before filling the bowl. Consider your dog's nutritional needs based upon age, health and activity level. Ideally, you should be concerned with balanced nutrition consisting of protein, vitamins and minerals. Ingredients on the labels are listed in descending order by weight, and you must know that there is a distinct quality difference in the industry definition between what constitutes beef, beef-by-products and beef meal.

Remember, too, that the aim of the dog food manufacturer is to get you the customer to buy their food, so foods are made to appeal to people as well. Bags are brightly colored to catch the consumer's eye. Pictures on can labels look like grandma's pot roast. Inside the package you may find cutely shaped bits in various meat and vegetable stained hues. What you might not know is that in reality what you are dishing out to Fido is cleverly disguised chicken feet and poultry intestines with some trace amounts of feathers that are allowed because they are "unavoidably" included during processing.

Is it any wonder why some dogs eat socks? *-March 2007*

Service Dogs and the Law

If you have any sort of job working with the public, it is vitally important that you and your employer fully understand the laws that apply to service and assistance animals. I say this because as a certified therapy dog handler, I often encounter situations where companies are in obvious need of education.

You first must need to know that I do not own the dog that I am currently training for therapy work. Even though she is not my pet, I have personally invested hundreds of dollars and thousands of hours of training into this dog. My hope is that this lovely animal will be certified to work in complex settings and eventually become a crisis response assistance animal. This means that this particular dog will be able to do the same type of work that the dogs who were present at 9/11 and the Virginia Tech shooting did in providing outlets for emotional response and calming people affected by the tragedies.

When this dog and I are out training, it is all work and no play. My job as her trainer, besides shaping her into the best possible animal, is to get her accustomed to as many situations as possible. Often times I do this by visiting places where there is a lot of human activity. Usually, we are well received and most people are great about letting us go about our business, Sometimes we make a quick trip through a department store to get accustomed to the sounds of the PA system and the hustle and bustle of people. When we do this not only are we not shopping, but my dog is well restrained in her carry bag and she wears industry identifiers.

On a recent outing to a department store where I would have expected better, we were ushered out before we even made it through the double doors. While I always respect and honor store policy, I usually take these negative responses as an opportunity to play "dumb" and find out more about their policies regarding assistance animals. This one particular employee told me that the store only allows service dogs that are accompanied by people with visible disabilities. And, they do not permit service dogs in training in the store, period. Then she gave me some song and dance about the food kiosk that is at the front of the store.

This store's policy violates the law. The first law that they are breaking is the federal Americans With Disabilities Act, which gives people with disabilities (visible and non-visible) the legal right to take animals in all areas open to the general public. "No Pet" policies do not apply to assistance animals, even in facilities that sell or prepare food. Furthermore, some individual state laws permit assistance dogs "in training" the same rights as those provided by the ADA.

If you work with the public you should learn about the laws that apply to assistance dogs. You should know that, by law, assistance dogs are not required to wear special items to identify that they are working, you are not permitted to ask someone to prove his or her disability, nor are you allowed to require proof that the assistance animal is certified. *–April 2008*

Book Review: *Dog Days at the White House*

As a child, I remember being fascinated by a dog book in my elementary school library. It was a book of pictures that had the most intriguing photograph on the front cover. It was of a man driving away in a snazzy sports car, and sitting beside him was a head of flowing blonde hair. Inside was a photo of the same man, but because of the different angle of the camera, the mysterious passenger was revealed to be an Afghan hound.

This began my love of dog books. I began collecting a few years ago, and I now have books on every dog-gone topic from puppy psychology to baking biscuits. My special collection has grown so large, in fact, that one of the rooms in my home now looks like a public library annex.

I love to spread the word about a good book, and I have this strange habit of playing the Furry Godmother by leaving dog books in places where I think they are needed. Recently, I added a book to the collection at the Claiborne Pell Center for International Affairs after noticing that there were shelves of books about politics and American history but there wasn't a single dog book to be found.

The book that I slipped from my tote bag onto the shelf when I thought no one was looking was Traphes Bryant's *Dog Days at the White House*. This book contains the drooling diary of the White

House kennel keeper during the terms of Presidents Truman to Nixon. It is the perfect book to add to a summer reading list during an election year because it not only gives fun details about dogs that soiled the carpets of our Presidential mansion, but it also gossips about some juicy behind-the-scenes secrets of the political and personal goings-on of America's first families.

Within the pages is an account of how President Kennedy asked to pet his dog Charlie while coping with the tension of the Cuban Missile Crisis, and how he insisted on being met by the dogs whenever his Presidential Helicopter landed on the White House lawn. There's also an account of LBJ's love for his beagles and how they helped him win the popular vote by wearing the campaign motto "LBJ for the USA" soldered to their collars.

Bryant's memoirs also include stories of puppies running rampant in the Oval Office; emergency visits from the vet, and complaints from one President about dog-hair on his dark suits. The really neat thing about this book is how it tricks the reader into unknowingly learning about American history.

I've never been a fan of political life, but this doggedly charming book had me begging to learn more about the dogs of Washington, both two-legged and four-legged. –*June 2008*

Starving Dog Art Exhibit

I've got a bone to pick. Recently I received a dog crate full of e-mail about the controversial artist Guillermo "Habacuc" Vargas. For those of you who don't know about the artist, he is the South American sensation who installed a starving street dog in his exhibit titled "Eres que lo lees" at a Nicaraguan art gallery. When I saw the pictures of the emaciated dog included in the e-mails, my first reaction was that of rabid-dog outrage.

However, my domesticated and sensible side advised me to do a bit of investigating and fact checking before passing a final judgment. I did this because I know that the Internet has become the modern storytelling medium for fueling witch-hunts and perpetuating urban legends. My investigation confirmed that the art exhibit was, in fact, real.

In October of 2007, Habacuc took a starving dog off of the streets and tied him with a short rope to the corner wall of an empty exhibit hall at the Códice gallery. The title of the work, "You are What You Read," was stenciled in dog food kibble on the wall above the starving dog. Crowds of visitors passed through the exhibit hall, but no one did anything to help the animal or stop the display of Vargas's "masterpiece."

I dug up a number of contradictory statements issued about the fate of the dog. The artist first declared that the dog died and would have "died anyway." Later the gallery owner claimed that the animal "escaped" after the first day. Critics of art have ignored the inhumane treatment of the animal altogether. Instead, they explain that the stories spun on the Internet are exactly the affirmation the contemporary artist was trying to elicit with his installation; this is alleged to be a commentary on how humanity blindly and unaffectedly walks by moral injustices every day and only becomes outraged when they later read about them in the morning paper.

As someone who deeply values art as commentary on society, I can appreciate the artist's message. However, I stand with hackles raised in strong opposition to his chosen medium. What's more, I cannot help but wonder how this world can ever become less vicious when even gentle-natured artists can commit such acts of indifference.

Vargas has been invited to compete in the 2008 Biennale showing in Honduras. There is an e-petition circulating, but because Vargas has received a private invitation, this growing list of names cannot stop his participation. Personally, I've chosen to growl by affixing my pawprint to the Universal Declaration for Animal Welfare. This proposal encourages worldwide improvement in the legislation that protects animals. *–May 2008*

Memorial Day is for Dogs

Last Monday we celebrated Memorial Day, the national day of remembrance for those men, women, and dogs who have died while serving our country. Yes, you read that right. Memorial Day is for dogs, too. Author Michael Lemish estimates that over 30,000 dogs have served in the U.S. military.

Throughout American history, many dogs of war have sacrificed their own lives in the process of saving human soldiers. Many armies throughout the world regularly include dogs as part of their battle strategy. The tradition began with Napoleon, who first used dogs for guard and sentry duty. Since then, the employment potential for dogs in the military has expanded tremendously.

Many people are already aware of the dog's keen ability to detect land mines and other explosive devices. Dogs were a vital part of military communications in early years. They not only served as messengers with notes strapped to their collars, but they also functioned as a means to run communications wires in thick brush, over rough terrain, and through narrow underground pipes. They were quick, efficient and enabled communications that might not have otherwise been achieved by their human counterparts.

The dog's keen hearing enabled the French to triangulate the location of German artillery bunkers by marking the dog's line of sight during night exercises. This same sense also allowed dogs to warn of approaching aircraft before the invention of radar. In American history, hearing and scent together proved very effective for locating a new type of enemy that concealed themselves in the jungle during the Vietnam conflict.

Dogs have also been central to search and rescue missions. A dog can scout out a wounded soldier, and in an interesting irony, carry that soldier's dog tags back to headquarters for the purpose of rapidly getting medical attention to seriously wounded soldiers in the field.

A National War Dogs memorial is still only in the planning process, but there is no denying that there are no creatures more loyal and courageous than the dogs that have given their lives in the name of defense. I thank those fallen heroes. *–June 2006*

Dog Rental Business

I think it is cool that some baby boomers are keeping dogs in their lives by becoming part-time pooch parents. My mom has some friends in Washington State who share a dog with another couple. When one couple is summering in another part of the world or taking exotic vacations, the other family keeps the dog, and vice versa. This seems to be a viable alternative for the members of our maturing population who would rather not be tied down by the responsibility of full-time dog ownership.

From what I understand, this system works pretty well for everyone involved. Pooch co-parents get the many emotional and physical benefits that accompany dog ownership. The dog fares well because even in this larger communal sphere there remains both environmental stability and familiar social bonds. Unfortunately, in our commercial society, whenever a new concept surfaces, there always seems to be a wolf who hijacks the idea and exploits it for money. Companies are popping up that provide "rental" dogs for the non-committal dog owner.

Want to impress a date? Feel lonely for companionship? Need to show visiting family members that you have a stable home? New companies are suggesting that Rover rental may be for you. These businesses work by charging an initial membership fee for a one or two days a month commitment to hire a dog. Of course, these canine custody days are subject to extra costs.

At first glance, this might seem like a pretty good idea to some. I mean if you can get by the insincerity of the premise, some might suggest that these rental dogs are never lacking for attention. Others might try to argue that dog-keeping based on convenience might be more fair to the dog than some committed ownerships in which the dog is left home alone for long periods of time.

The biggest problem with the rental scheme, however, lies in the fact that dogs need stability. It normally takes as long as a month for a dog to become adjusted to the expectations of a household. One-night stands at different locations are bound to cause problems with toilet training and basic household manners. America's over-populated animal shelters already tell us that behavioral problems are inevitable with dogs that are shuffled from person to person.

Another problem arises with the fact that the greatest benefits in our relationships with dogs lie in the intensity of the bond that we share with a particular animal. Basically, the stronger the connection we share with our creature comforts, the greater the emotional, social, and physical benefits we experience.

Fortunately, some states have passed laws that prohibit pet rentals. This legislation is intended to promote public health and safety and is good for humans and canines alike.

As far as dogs are concerned, there is no substitute for stability and commitment. If you are unable to provide both of these but still long for single-serving Fido fixes, consider volunteering at the local shelter where there are no membership fees. *–July 2008*

Pet-conomic Crisis

I just finished reading an article in one of my favorite doggy magazines about how the veterinary community has just launched a study to figure out why there has been a dramatic drop in the frequency of vet visits over the last couple of years. Leave it to some scientists who must never leave their laboratories to think that they actually need to conduct such a study. For me, the modest mutt who spends time walking around in the real world, the answer is as obvious as the nose on my muzzle.

I mean no disrespect, but I think that somebody needs to put a sticky note on the laboratory door that says: "economic crisis." It just seems obvious that during financial hard times, people feel forced to make difficult choices and renegotiate where they spend what little extra money they have. Sometimes this means that they stretch out visits to the vet, or they wait to see if a minor problem becomes a major one before seeking medical care. Some people are even turning to less expensive health alternatives instead of using traditional vet care.

To be sure, the modern economic crisis has taken a toll on pets in general. Shelters and rescue organizations have reported a record number of pets being surrendered because families are forced to vacate their homes due to foreclosure, or because they simply can't afford to keep them. As insidious as it sounds, needing to surrender the family dog due to crisis is a very harsh and unfortunate reality for a growing number of people.

The more the economy continues to spiral downward, the worse it gets for domestic pets. Stephen Zawistowski, vice-president of ASPCA programs explains, "As households across the country are caught in the economic downturn, an estimated 500,000 to one million cats and dogs are at risk of becoming homeless." The irony of this crisis is that there is no better therapist, confidante or crying towel to help a person through ruff times than a faithful pet.

This holiday season, if you have a family member or friend who has a dog and might also be feeling economically strained, consider giving them a gift that supports their pet. Instead of buying them a mindless dust collector or a gift card for a restaurant that they'll never use, consider giving them a bag of dog food. Better yet, perhaps purchase a modest gift certificate for routine services such as grooming or veterinary care. The idea is to give them something that will enable them to enjoy their pet in the upcoming year. I guarantee this will be the best gift under the tree.

Trust me, people love receiving gifts of any kind for their pooches at holiday time. I know this because I once saw a tug of war break out between two people over a squeaky toy that I brought to a howliday party Yankee swap. *–December 2010*

Chapter 6: Furballs of Fun

"The greatest pleasure of a dog is that you may make a fool of yourself with him, and not only will he not scold you, but he will make a fool of himself, too" - *Samuel Butler*

Photo by Thelma Laliberte

These Cold Noses That Warm Our Hearts

Cancer Detecting Dogs

It has been long known that dogs offer an array of physical, emotional and social benefits to people. Humankind's best friend is now digging its way into medicine. When I think about the dog's capacity to use its nose as a tool for diagnosing cancer, I cannot help but ask: Is there a dog-ter in the house?

Believe it or not, the first reported case of a dog detecting cancer in humans goes back to 1984 when a 44 year-old woman went to see her dermatologist because her Border Collie-Doberman mix kept sniffing and even tried to bite a mole off of her thigh. The skin growth turned out to be a malignant melanoma.

Since then, the idea that dogs could sniff out cancer has both intrigued and baffled the medical community. Scientists aren't exactly sure what causes the dog to be able to detect cancer, but they do know that dogs do not need to see a malignant lesion in order to respond to the presence of cancerous cells. This means that the dog's sniffer can also be used to detect lung and breast cancer.

Trainers have teamed up with scientists to properly train dogs to specifically detect malignant cells. The first dog formally trained to do this was a Schnauzer named George. George was taught to identify in-vitro malignant melanoma by a dermatologist who was teamed up with a police dog trainer. To train for cancer identification, the pair used simple detection-dog training methods like those used to train for search and rescue work.

Formal scientific studies have been conducted in recent years to test the dog's success rate for detecting cancer in containers filled with urine samples. Several samples were placed on the floor and trained cancer detection dogs evaluated the samples. Not surprisingly, the dogs consistently identified the urine sample from the patient with bladder cancer.

Typically, cancer-sniffing dogs get very active and excited upon identifying malignancy. They may jump around or get over-active. But this is not always the case. One of my fellow dog loving friends has a Boxer who has not had any formal melanoma detection training, yet he has identified cancer in people by refusing to move his nose once he finds a location of curiosity on the body. Talk about getting a pet-scan!

When I think about the various ways in which the dog is being used in the field of medicine, I am amazed. Seizure detection and glucose level detection dogs are just a few of the ways that dogs are already diplomats in the medical community. I look forward to the day when my yearly visit to the doctor's office includes being inspected by a cold nose. –*September 2009*

Pooch-inality Test

My obsession with dogs has reached a new level. I say this because I recently found myself taking an on-line pooch personality quiz to find out what kind of dog I would be. I'm a self-admitted pawsaholic who just can't seem to get enough of the furry stuff. However, it is clear that I'm not the only person who has crazy imaginings about my life as a dog. The simple fact that I actually found a personality test that would match my traits with a particular breed of dog means that I'm not the only squeaky-toy in cyberspace.

I found it interesting to answer the seven questions on the quiz "What Kind of Dog Would You Be?" The questions ranged from how I treat my friends to my feelings about exercise and there wasn't one dog-specific question on the list. I gave much thought to my answers and tried to be as objective and honest about myself as I possibly could so that I could feel confident about the accuracy of the outcome.

As I pressed the "calculate" button, I had imaginings of being identified as the majestic Saluki that hunted Gazelle in ancient Persia. I thought of myself as the small but mighty Maltese that lounged on velvet pillows in the homes of European aristocrats. I even fantasized about being the dignified Great Dane, a breed that was promoted from hunting to leading coaches because of its distinguished prance.

I found myself to be sadly disappointed when the results came back German Shepherd. "This can't be right," I mused to myself. My folks had a number of Shepherds over the years, and all I could remember was every one of them being overly bonded to one family member, being constantly underfoot and needlessly whining about everything. Sure, I loved their intelligence and athletic beauty, but my ears went back at the thought of being a needy German

Shepherd.

My mind quickly changed after I read the description that was provided with the results: "The German Shepherd is a workaholic. Intent on business, this loyal breed is always on patrol. Mental and physical exercise both appeal equally to the German Shepherd, and her intelligence is further enhanced by her dedicated nature. When it comes to dependability, the German Shepherd has the market cornered."

I was amazed by how perfectly this doggy description depicted my personality, and I suddenly envisioned myself as a canine heroine in the US Cavalry partnered up with the iconic Rin Tin Tin. I smiled at the fantasy of having my own star next to his on Hollywood boulevard.

Taking this personality quiz was really fun and in the process I learned some new things about myself and about the dogs that I love. But just so we are clear, you should know that in my life as a German Shepherd, I have perfectly manicured toenails and I wear a pink studded leather collar with a matching leash. *–June 2008*

The Dog's Sense of Justice

My two dogs were having a play date with a friend's two dogs last weekend when I observed a most interesting behavior. Three dogs were playing tug-of-war while one was sitting on the sidelines like a referee. When one of the tug-of-war players became overly rough by unfairly tugging another dog by the ear instead of pulling the toy, the referee pooch stepped in. She nudged the sore sport with her muzzle, gave a loud, scolding "yarf" and then went back to her place on the sidelines as the tug game resumed.

I was amazed by what had just happened, and it got me to thinking more deeply about the dog's capacity for justice. I wondered: can dogs really know the difference between what is right and what is wrong?

I answered my own question immediately. Of course they can. Ask any dog owner who has just caught their dog raiding the garbage can or chewing a hole in the sofa cushion. Most, if not all owners would say that their dog knows that it has done something wrong just by the look of worry or regret that it shows on its face.

Until recently, science has not been so easy to agree that the hidden life of dogs is rich with possibility and scientists are just beginning to acknowledge that dogs experience many of the same feelings that humans experience. As absurd as it seems to anyone who has ever lived with a dog, the scientific revolution in the seventeenth century set the stage for viewing animals as dumb beasts with a strictly limited ability to think and feel.

Fortunately, the laboratory seems to be catching up with our experience of reality in the new millennium. Science has claimed the discovery of a wide range of animal emotions that include joy, sorrow, anger and even embarrassment. What's more, new conclusions now suggest that dogs possess a rudimentary morality as well as an understanding of fairness and justice. A study from the National Academy of Sciences found that a dog might refuse to play ball if it thinks that it is being treated unfairly.

Like humans, dogs are social animals. Their cooperation is based upon a set of social rules. Fair behavior, or that which is just and right, occurs within this social scheme of what is deemed acceptable. Granted, this is a much simpler form of moral behavior than that which we understand in human terms, but thinking from the perspective of human superiority is the very problem that imposes limits on our ability to fully understand the animal realm.

I like to think in terms of potentiality when it comes to the secret life of my dogs. I suspect that the canine mind may be much more intricate than we humans can fathom. As to the question of an evolved sense of canine righteousness: I cannot be sure, but it is highly unlikely that any dog I know would turn out to be the immoral mastermind behind a Ponzi dogbone scheme. *–March 2009*

A Dog's Amazing Senses

X-men, step aside, we don't need your super hero strength. Batman, tell Robin to put away his red tights and stay home; there is a new action hero on the block. You may not know it, but there are real Underdogs living all around us.

Growing up, I remember reading comic books and watching shows on television that featured characters like Spiderman and Wonder Woman. These were fantasy characters with many superhuman qualities that I childishly dreamed were real. Imagine being able to see through walls? Wouldn't it be cool to leap tall buildings in a single bound?? It's a bird! It's a plane!!

It's a dog!!! Until I began working on my doctorate, I never gave much thought to the super human senses that my dog has. Although scientists disappointingly tell us that dogs can't fully see Technicolor, I say who cares? Dogs don't need to match socks or stop the car at traffic lights. The simple truth is that compared to me, my dog has super-strength sight. For starters, my dog has significantly much better night vision than any human. Dog also have a greater sight radius than people. A sheepdog, for example, has a 180-degree radius of vision – even with his hair hanging over its eyes. In other words, the dog can see from over its left shoulder all the way above and around to its right shoulder without having to turn its head.

My dog also has superhero hearing. We're talking supersonic Siryn ears. A dog can hear clearly at 30 feet what we humans can barely hear at 5 feet, and they can hear ultrasonic waves. Pointy-eared dogs can listen better than floppy-eared dogs, but either one still hears dog years better than me on my best ear-wax free day.

Let's not forget the most famous of the dog's crime-fighting features: its sniffer. Compared to the meek 5 million scent cells that we people have inside of our noses, the dog has up to 195 million or more depending on the breed. A Basset hound has 125 million and the German shepherd has a whopping 200 million olfactory cells. Scent is the most widely studied of all the dog's senses, and research estimates that the dog's Incredible Hulk-ing nose can detect one tiny little drop of blood in 5 liters of water.

I normally don't like to tell people, but I think that my little black furry dog might be leading a secret double-life as Superman. The other night I swear he used his X-ray vision to see a mouse in the wall, though it is more likely that his growl-woof was because he heard the little rascal scurrying around in the 3:00 am silence. The next day we set a trap and evacuated the unwelcome rodent, thus eliminating the need to borrow a cat. My dog, my hero. *–October 2009*

My Dog Went to Harvard

When I sent in the application for my youngest dog to participate in the Canine Cognition Laboratory at Harvard University a few months ago, I honestly did not expect to be contacted. The truth is that although I think of my darling as best in show in my doghouse, I realize that she's not the brightest biscuit in the cookie box. In signing up, I was not convinced that she would make the grade as college material, but I was hopeful.

When I learned that the research staff invited my pooch to participate in the study, I was really excited even though I was imagining my dog as comparable to the character Elle Woods in the film "Legally Blonde." When I confirmed our meeting, I made up my mind that even if she flunked out, a visit to Harvard University with my bubble headed Cavalier would be nothing less than a fun adventure.

The Canine Cognition Lab is based in the school's psychology department, and the researchers there are studying the dog's mind. Through a series of non-invasive experiments, they are interested in learning more about dog thoughts and feelings. Among other things, specific tests are designed to investigate how a dog solves problems, recognizes patterns of sound and reflects on what is known and unknown.

Interestingly, the dog's brain and the human brain are shockingly similar. Many of the medications prescribed to people for psychological conditions are also given to dogs to treat the same mental conditions. In the Harvard Study, the overriding goals are to expand what is known about canine intelligence and to somehow connect what is learned from these studies with dogs to better understand the human mind.

When we arrived with wagging tails for the scheduled one-hour appointment, the research assistant assured me that heightened intelligence is not necessarily required for dog test subjects, but good temperament around strangers and a love for treats is a must.

To be sure, the lab experience was furballs of fun! I stayed with my dog the entire time and I was an active participant in the two experiments conducted that day. The first test involved recognizing body cues and facial gestures. The second trial had to do with problem solving and the dog's understanding the principles of physics. Both experiments were videotaped so the researcher could make careful notes and gather valuable data at a later time.

To my surprise, when our scheduled lab time ended, the researchers invited us to come back to participate in some of the other tests. They also presented my four-legged scholar with a nifty diploma. She's been flashing her sheepskin to the other dogs in the house, and it is so annoying that I'm beginning to wonder what the starting salary is for a dog with an Ivy League education in this job market. *–July 2010*

Reflexive Resonance

No doubt, the majority of the academic community thinks that this dog-crazy scholar is a few biscuits short of a box. Whenever I dare to express my beliefs that dogs have emotions, can think on their own and have the capacity to distinguish right from wrong, my experience is that most of the traditional learned community roll their eyes and think that I should be dropped off at the dog pound.

On the other paw, the holistic scientific community sits at my side when I throw the ball about canine sentience and a dog's sensing ability on a metaphysical level. I have written previously about the dog's ability to know when its owners are coming home through morphic field resonance. I have a new idea that builds both on Sheldrake's morphic resonance and the fact that quantum physics tells us that we are constantly exchanging molecules with everything in our environment. I call my concept the canine quality of "reflexive resonance."

Reflexive resonance is the idea that dogs can mirror their owner's medical conditions. My hypothesis is not the same thing as zoonosis, whereby animals and people can pass diseases such as rabies and staph infections between one another. Rather, reflexive resonance deals with the echoing of more profound pain and illness that simply cannot be explained by the traditional medical model.

I first encountered this phenomenon when I was a Master's degree student and a fellow classmate shared with me the story of her sister's illness. She told me that a few years earlier, her sister had been diagnosed with a very rare form of cancer and was undergoing treatment for her affliction. Six months into her sister's treatment, her beloved dog fell ill. After some tests, the veterinarian informed my classmate's sister that her dog had been stricken by the same rare type of cancer that she herself was battling. Blessedly, the sister survived cancer, but her dog ultimately died. My classmate assured me that to this day her sister believes that her dearly loved dog took her cancer away and sacrificed its own life in order to spare hers.

Since then, I've been listening more closely when people with back problems have told me about their dog's slipped disc or when people with ulcers tell me they feed their dog a sensitive stomach diet. My ears stood up recently as a runner explained how she was rehabilitating her dog after having knee surgery because she herself had undergone the same medical procedure earlier this year.

Surely, I'll need a Great Dane of evidence before I introduce my hypothesis to the academic community without worry that they'll tie me up in a doggy straight-jacket. Meanwhile, I'll continue to sit up and beg for any tales of reflexive resonance that people are willing to share. *–September 2007*

What's in a Dog Name?

Last week, I met a dog that was named Lisa. This was a first for me. In my 30 years of working with dogs, I have never before known a dog that was named Lisa. She's a fun, sweet and smart Wirehaired Griffin. But seriously folks, what is the deal with naming a dog Lisa? Inquiring minds want to know.

People have close relationships with their dogs, and often consider them to be important members of the family. For some people, the family dog may act as a substitute child, brother, sister or lifelong companion. What's more, a dog represents both an extension and reflection of ourselves, a fact that makes choosing the perfect name as important as selecting the perfect breed.

It is no joke to say that bestowing a name on a dog we call our very own is some serious business. I've known people to even go so far as to change the name of an adopted dog because they didn't like the moniker that their new furry family member arrived with. This idea of dog names got me to thinking about all the dogs I have known.

I've met my share of Maxes, and seen several Sams. I've known a number of Nicks, a bunch of Baileys, and many Mollies. Author Stanley Coren remarks that the top 10 most popular names for male and female dogs have remained constant over the past decade. He says the most popular name for males is Max, and Princess for females. But clearly I'm not interested in those popular names. Let's face it: Lisa is not exactly "everyday."

I have known people to name their dogs after musicians: Jagger, Chopin, Ozzy, Shaynia, and Nas. Sports stars are also fair game: Jeeter, Schilling, Pedro, Bruin, Rusty and Dale. Movie names make more than the marquee: Butch, Sundance, Hutch, Babe, Damien, and Cujo. Cartoon characters evidently aren't just for kids anymore: Stitch, Bruce, Gizmo, Odie, Pebbles and Dino. My own beloved, in fact, is named after a character from the television series "Law and Order."

So, back to Lisa. I wondered: could she be the namesake of the Mona Lisa? Was it that she is named for actress Lisa Kudrow? Singer Lisa Loeb? I did have the occasion to ask her owner, and discovered that she's named after the notoriously famous Lisa from "The Simpsons" cartoon. Now that I think about it, her name couldn't be more perfect: She's smart, she's sweet, she's fun, and the hair sticks up on the top of her head. *–May 2006*

Dog Cookies

The holiday season is upon us again. Like many of you, I am about to become a slave to my oven. Among many of my baking tasks, I will need to make fourteen dozen cookies in preparation for the annual cookie swap with my girlfriends. This is no ordinary swap, however, since our exchange includes a contest that names a reigning cookie queen for the upcoming year.

Competing in the cookie contest is serious business among the girls. Each lady plans in secret all year long for the big bake-off, trying to make the perfect cookie that will win best in show. Sadly, I have never been top dog in the competition. I usually either use an old recipe that somehow doesn't come when it is called, or I try a new recipe for the first time that rolls over and plays dead. So, I have decided to try something different this year: I'm baking dog cookies.

Thinking about cookies and holiday cheer reminds me of a dog story.

One year long ago, my mom and I decided to put together doggy bags of cookies for all of our poochie friends at holiday time. We went to a gourmet store and bought heaps of dog treats that had been made to look just like commercial brands of people cookies. We were preparing our assembly line of snacks on the counter, but we had both stepped out of the kitchen for a moment.

When mom returned, she saw dad tossing what appeared to be an Oreo in his mouth. She stood watching, unsure about how to tell him that he just ate a dog biscuit. "They're a little dry," he said as he popped another goody between his teeth. When I returned upon the scene, my mother was laughing so hard that she had tears streaming down her face and my dad was gulping milk like he was trying to antidote poison. Needless to say, he never stole food off of the counter again.

Dog biscuits gained their popularity after World War II when a shortage of metal in the United States caused the production of canned dog food to sharply decline. Today, dog snacks are an integral part of the 15 billion dollar pet food industry. They can provide good supplements to regular meals, since healthy treats are rich with vitamins and minerals. However, dog food expert Liz Palika warns, "Treats loaded with sugar are very poor nutrition." With this in mind, I dug up this bone-delicious recipe.

Blue Ribbon Dog Biscuits

2 3/4 cups whole-wheat flour, 1/2 cup powdered milk, 1 tsp. salt, 1/4 tsp garlic powder,
1 egg, 6 tbs. vegetable oil, 8-10 tbs. water, 2 small jars strained baby food (beef, chicken, lamb, or liver). Preheat your oven to 350 degrees. Mix all ingredients together in a large bowl and knead for about 3 minutes. Roll out to 1/2 inch thick. Cut into shapes and place biscuits on an ungreased baking sheet. Bake for 20-25 minutes. Cool, wrap and keep refrigerated.

I don't know how well my cookies will go over with the swap contest judges, but I'll bet their dogs will be grateful little elves. – *December 2006*

The Canine Con

I'm always hearing stories about how people are easily tricked by their dogs. One friend of mine admits that his dog pretends to have a bathroom emergency just so she can get the cookie reward when he lets her back in the house. He laughs as he tells the story of his dog dashing outside to do nothing but run back over to the door so she can come in for a treat. The best part is that he confesses that sometimes she'll do this three times in a row before he catches on.

I'm convinced that the average dog is far more calculating than most owners would ever suspect, and I believe that many dogs do an incredible job of getting what they want by turning into little con artists. Luckily, I consider myself too smart of an alpha dog to fall for those kinds of dog tricks, so in my pack the pooches are forced to practice their swindling skills on each other.

I observed one such scam recently when my youngest was happily gnawing on a bone that my oldest decided she wanted. Although we have a box overflowing with toys, she wanted THAT bone. First, she tried walking right up to the young one and rudely attempted to pull the bone right out of her mouth. In terms of doggy manners, this is a big no-no. The little one rightfully growled, and the older one properly backed off.

When that didn't work, the older one cleverly tried creating a diversion by running over to the door and giving a bark at the imaginary doorbell ringing. You see, in the dog social structure, once a dog looks away from anything that it has, then that item becomes fair game for any other pack member to take. When the younger one heard the bark, she merely looked casually in the direction of the door with the bone tightly clenched in her teeth. Apparently she had fallen for this trick before, and she wasn't going to fall for it again.

Then I saw the light go on over the older one's head as she dashed off to get one of the identical looking, but much smaller bones from the toy basket. She trotted back with the bone and plopped herself down next to the young one. I saw her half-heartedly begin mouthing the small bone while she nonchalantly edged it closer and closer to the bigger bone that her young friend was chewing. In an instant, she pulled a dog bone bait and switch. She pushed the small bone right on top of the big bone and while the young dog momentarily glanced at the two bones, the older dog picked up the bigger bone by "mistake" before walking away.

Sadly, the younger dog seemed to have absolutely no idea that she had just been duped. After her success, I truly hope my canine con artist doesn't think that she'll be able to pull a switch-a-roo with her squeaky hamburger at the next family cook out. – *August 2010*

Dogs

A couple of weeks ago, I walked into my parent's house to find my nearly sixty year-old mother lying flat on her back on the floor. She had a squeaker toy in one hand and she was passing it back and forth through the air over her stomach as her little dog hurdled from one side of her abdomen to the other.

"What on earth are you doing?" I asked, both glad that she didn't need me to call for an ambulance and dying for a reasonable explanation for this ridiculous scene. "Exercising," she replied with a stone serious look as she continued to pass the squeaky bunny. It took a second to register that she was joking because I wasn't expecting this reply, but then the both of us belly laughed so hard that we almost peed on the floor without hitting the newspaper.

"When the doctor suggested that you get more exercise, I don't think that he had this in mind," I giggled. "What?" she replied with that doggy's got a bone grin. "Well I am working up a sweat and my arm's getting tired," she added.

A recent study conducted at Queens University in Belfast, Ireland has determined that dog owners are healthier than cat owners. The study suggested that this was due to the fact that dog owners get more physical exercise and have a higher level of social interaction during physical activity. In short, doggercising creates a buffer to stress that leads to healthier living.

I'm not the athletic type, but I do love to get out and have fun with my dog. Whenever the weather allows, I take my dog for a two-mile walk through the city. On weekends in summer, she wears her doggy life-jacket and we go dog paddling together. This week, we've been running around playing "tag" in the backyard until it gets dark.

"Sorry," I told my mom, "But I don't think that waving the squeaky bunny qualifies as exercise. Perhaps exercise for the dog, but certainly not for you."

Still, I could see that mom and her pooch were having fun, and watching their unconventional "exercise program" got me to thinking about how I might be able to integrate my own pup into my daily yoga routine.

I did some investigating and found out that it's called "doga," and it's the latest rage on the west coast. In this innovative form of exercise, people partner with their dogs while holding various poses that strengthen the body and mind. Sometimes the dogs integrate with the stretch, and sometimes they support the pose.

I tried some doga stretches at home with my own pooch. After a little practice and a lot of laughs, we both found it to be great fun. I'd love to teach mom these cool new moves, but she's currently recovering from a sports injury. Apparently, waving the squeaky bunny gave her tennis elbow. –*July 2007*

Traveling With Dogs

My dog and I just returned from an exotic travel adventure. After spending an exhilarating week rolling in the sand and dog-paddling in the surf on the Yucatan coast, I can see why the celebrity lifestyle includes the luxury of vacationing with four-legged friends.

Without a doubt, my dog is the best traveling companion that I have ever had. She is never late, doesn't complain about the food, and always digs into any adventure. I am amazed by how easily she adapts to new experiences, and our most recent journey together has made me realize just how cool it can be to travel with a pet. To be sure, my pup and I are already interstate road-trippers, but one of the exciting aspects of our Mexican adventure was the fun of flying the dog-friendly skies!

Fortunately, my 9-month old puppy only weighs 12 pounds, so she easily met the weight and size restrictions imposed by the airlines that enabled her to fly right beside me in the cabin of the plane. In preparation for earning her wings, I had my puppy practice staying in her airline-approved travel bag for periods of time every day so that she would feel relaxed on travel day. We also got our paws on the necessary puppy travel papers, such as proof of vaccinations and a veterinarian approved health certificate, which are required for the transport of live animals between the U.S. and Mexico.

On travel day, we brought my suitcase and our reservation information to the check-in counter at the airport where we also received our seat and "under-the-seat in front of me" assignments. We went together into the security area, and just like the two-legged passengers, my dog had to take off her jacket and the metal buckle that she was wearing. While her carrier was being x-rayed, I presented our identification and boarding passes to the security attendants. As I carried her through the metal detector, I made notice of how her wagging tail got more than a few smiles from onlookers.

By the time we boarded the plane, my pet was settled inside her travel bag and gnawing on a super-sized chewy that I hoped would keep her busy for our four-hour flight south of the border. As we took off, I crossed my fingers that she wouldn't cry or get airsick, and I was soon delighted by how calm she was. She never made a fuss, and at one point I could see that she was flopped on her back and sleeping with her legs stuck straight in the air. I noticed this because her snoring was almost drowning out the sound of the in-flight movie that I was watching.

When we did finally arrive at our destination, a woman who was exiting the plane noticed my little darling. As she walked past us, I heard her remark to her husband, "Oh, did you know there was a dog on this plane? That dog was quieter than that annoying kid behind us who kept screaming and pawing at the back of my seat." This makes me think that maybe dogs should fly free. –*January 2008*

He, She or It?

I'm having an argument with the academic community. Recently, I submitted a journal article for review by a group of scientific types in the field of social work. For those of you who are not familiar with this type of publication, basically what happens is a work of writing is rigorously evaluated by a group of experts in a scientific field. These esteemed individuals must approve all aspects of the article for intellectual integrity before it is published.

The scholarly article that I have authored is about the role of the dog in the family system. While there are many, many articles written about the human family as a system, there are very few, if any, which include a central reference to the family dog. For the greater academic community, my writing is barking up an unfamiliar tree.

Nevertheless, the reviewers' responses are favorable thus far, and I'm pleased that they have invited me to revise the article. However there is one minor sticking point that is causing a fight at the dog park. Here's the problem: Throughout the article, whenever I refer to the dog, I use a "he/she" orientation. The academics have commented that this is poor grammar and suggested that I should be referring to the dog as an "it" entity. Sadly, from a grammatical point of view they are correct. This is one of those English language nuances that has yet to change with the passing of time.

My contention, however, is that referring to a dog as "it" is politically incorrect. As far as I'm concerned, my dog is an emotional and intellectual entity that should not be subordinated to the status of object. My toaster is an "it." A dog dish is an "it." In my view, my sentient companion is definitely NOT an "it."

This is an era where there is a great deal of focus on the language that is used to describe our roles as dog "keepers." Currently, there is a great debate as to whether we humans should continue to be called "owners" or if the language should change to "guardians" or "stewards." This word dispute has far reaching consequences for views of animals in society as well as for animal rights and human responsibilities. We all know that cultural concepts and language evolves over time. There was a time, for example, when certain people were abhorrently referred to as "it." There was also a time that calling something "cool" didn't mean that it was hot with popularity.

Through this experience, it occurred to me that this grammatical undercurrent might be partly to blame for the undermining of the position of dogs in the cultural scheme. Personally, I find this whole "it" business to be quite unsettling, especially coming from the intellectually enlightened. –*August 2008*

Overweight Dog?

I am living proof that old dogs can learn new tricks. I'm not ashamed to admit that every doggone day I learn something new. My story begins several weeks ago when Mrs. Martin asked me if I thought her young Boston Terrier mix, Buffy, was pregnant.

I looked at the pudgy pooch and thought to myself that she could definitely use a diet. I tried to respond to the question with logic and tact. "Well, has she been in heat?" Mrs. Martin told me that she hadn't seen any blood, and knowing that she doesn't miss a trick, I confidently assured Mrs. M that it was highly unlikely that her four-legged friend was in a family way. "Too many cookies," I told Mrs. M as I launched into my doggie-needs-a-diet lecture.

Statistics show that last year alone the American pet food industry raked in an amazing $14.7 BILLION. I shudder to think about how many calories that translates into. Overeating and under-exercising – the American predicament – are also the primary causes of obesity in dogs. Think about how our lifestyle affects our pets. While we work all day, our bored hounds lounge on the sofa. When we come home, we quickly fill the void by loving them with food. Then, after we tend to our family, home, and finish going through 87 e-mails, we find ourselves simply too spent to take the dog for a few laps around the block.

Poor Mrs. Martin. My sermon continued on about how being overweight can lead to very costly knee and back injuries. By the way, for you readers who don't know: Your dog has kneecaps. I went on and ON to Mrs. M about how, like people, overweight dogs run the risk of developing diabetes, digestive tract, skin, heart and a host of other serious health problems.

I suggested that she refer to the Body Conditioning System guide at www.Purina.com to see pictures of what industry professionals recommend Buffy's best body should look like. I also advised taking walks and cutting back on what we earlier agreed were too many snacks.

Recently, Mrs. Martin told me that she is the proud grandmother of three beautiful puppies, and this old dog learned something new. I learned that I should have asked Mrs. M if Buffy had gone outside without a chaperone. Clearly, my lecture about "silent heats" and the benefits of spaying and neutering would have been much less embarrassing. *–August 2006*

CPSIA information can be obtained
at www.ICGtesting.com
Printed in the USA
BVHW041954021219
565426BV00009B/177/P